IT'S PULL TO GO UP

Jeff Gray

Burnt Ash Publishing

First published in Great Britain in 2020

Burnt Ash Publishing
A division of Burnt Ash Developments Limited
86-90 Paul Street
London
EC2A 4NE

Printed by Elcograf
Typeset in Bookman Old Style, titles in Impact, captions in Acumin

ISBN 978-1-9162161-5-0

A CIP Catalogue for this book is available from the British Library

Contents

Foreword

When my father, Jeff Gray, died in 2016, I knew little of his early life, or his wartime experiences. Like many others, he had been reluctant to speak of them.

Going through his papers I found a worn file entitled, *It's Pull To Go Up,* containing several hundred typed pages, mostly ordered, and several old exercise books in my father's characteristic handwriting, that had been buried in a box in the wardrobe. It soon became clear that he had written an autobiographical account of his career as a pilot.

Reading through these papers I realised that there is so much that I didn't know about him. I have found it a fascinating story as I am sure you will. I have ordered the papers as best I can and resolved some inconsistencies, otherwise the story is entirely his own.

Robert Gray
December 2016

Preface

I am indebted to an unknown and waggish colleague for my book title. When I left the Blue Funnel Line[1] to go to the Middle East, he hung a notice on the control column of the VC10 simulator: 'Jeff', it said, 'it's pull to go up and push to go down'.

I am also indebted to my typist. I set out to write about aviation and flying training and my wife undertook the typing. In setting the scene, Mrs Garden got included, and my wife liked that. Mrs Garden brought others in her train and so changed the whole nature of the book.

Aviation today is propelled forward, not so much by its history and the hard-won lessons of the past, as by modern technology, and it was the first to benefit by the knowledge gained from space exploration. It remains, however, a long, hard haul for its participants and, for as long as we rely on airflow over the wings to stay airborne, many of its basic truths will remain.

The same was also true of Mrs Garden's beliefs and, in the end, her views carried the day, although it was a close-run thing for a time.

Jeff Gray
1983

---

1 BOAC, later, British Airways.

All things are bonny

It was never my intention to become a pilot. It just so happened that the recruiting centre combined Army and Air Force and the Army man was having his day off. The Air Force officer who interviewed me decided, for reasons of his own, to recruit me to his branch of the service and I was readily persuaded.

It was a little more difficult for me to get a day off to attend. At that time Scottish rural workers were not over-blessed with holidays, or holiday entitlement. I worked, however, for the best boss I ever had. Jake was farm grieve at Potts of Rayne and never forgot that he, like the rest of us, was an employee. So he treated us well and, in addition, was a marvellous, hard-working bloke with a great sense of humour and a real gent. As a result, he could drive us as hard as he liked and, led by Dod Perrie, we flew at the work, striving always to be first in the district to finish each task. We felt we had a reputation to keep and Jake turned a blind eye when we broke something or a horse bolted, or, on one terrible occasion, when we didn't hear the alarm and he had to call us.

I don't think it is possible, now, to convey the right impression of how serious life was then and how strict the conditions of employment. You were entitled to one day's holiday a year, on New Year's Day; which the Scots always had a thing about anyway, and a further day at term time every six months. If you were intending to continue in the job, you were not expected to take the latter holiday, only if you were moving on. In addition, you could ask for a day to attend the feeing market, the hiring fair further south, if you had decided to move, or had not been asked to stay.

The feeing markets have gone. They were held in places like Inverurie and Insch and Huntly. We farm servants dressed ourselves up in our blue serge suits and bonnets and Sunday boots and there was no mistaking us as we congregated in the square or market place. The farmers seeking labourers walked about among us, just as easily recognisable for what they were, judging each one as they might have judged a Clydesdale horse or a fat bullock. I would not have been too surprised to be handled or prodded like a horse, which was the equivalent of showing one's teeth.

So it was likely that Jake had given me one of those days, as I was old enough to join up. I had been too young for the Territorials and so had missed out on the free kilt and, of course, I was much too young for the militia men. They were the twenty-one-year-olds and had been the first to go. The Terriers were not called, to my surprise, till later and then seemed to spend their time accommodated in various drill halls in the district. It was felt locally that they might have been better employed at home, in fact, they were soon gone. Gone, as it happened, with the British Expeditionary Force to France, not seen again till the survivors were freed from the cage at the end of the war. The Blitzkrieg released by the Germans, that fateful May in 1940, swept through them like a scythe through corn.

And so, when I was old enough, I went to join the Gordons. Today, we can't call them the Gay Gordons. It is no loss; the title never suited them, recruited as they were largely from the North-East, as gaiety is not a characteristic of these people. The harsh climate and the struggle to make a living is not productive of gaiety.

Although ours was not a family of any great traditions, as tradition and humble origins do not sit easily together, I had, nevertheless, absorbed something of the tradition of service from my surroundings. The house was full of photographs of men in uniform, in rather stiff, formal poses, generally kilted or wearing the Anzac slouch hat and knee breeches, and so these pictures which were well known to me in my childhood, although the actual people were not. My mother, now in her eighties, still has these pictures, but they are not now in evidence. They have discreetly disappeared.

My Air Force friend described the army life, which seemed very like that which I was leading; short on creature comfort and long on hard graft. The RAF, on the other hand, slept between sheets. I could see that he had me assessed correctly. However when it came to selecting the particular branch of the service I should join we ran into our first difficulty. Although I had listened carefully to all he had to say about the many attractive slots they needed to fill, the RAF meant only one thing to me: pilot. I don't think he had actually seen me as aircrew material up to this point, but it was the sticking point and, perhaps with a trace of reluctance, that is what he put down on the form. It was spoilt slightly for me as the category was pilot/navigator, not separated out in any way, but linked together. In fact, it turned out later that the navigator category was something of a hurdle and those good at maths found the first word deleted. I was fairly secure there; maths was not my best subject.

I remember too, there was a medical. Here I felt that I had nothing to fear. I had inherited the slight, but wiry, build of the Alexanders, along with their prominent nose, and missed out on the stocky broad-backed figure of the Grays. I've often thought that the hard physical work tilling the rich soil of Buchan when I was at such an early age and obviously not built for it, perhaps had stunted my growth. My father believed that my feet were too much turned under and, had it not been for that, I would have been of a decent height. I had, however, been blessed with perhaps the best inheritance of all; good health derived from hardy stock.

The medical officer was not impressed. I could pass easily each of his tests, taken individually, but the whole was not put together in a pleasing manner and I got the distinct impression that he was displeased. Over the next forty years, I have undergone more medicals than I care to think about and I've often seen that same look. It was only latterly that they seemed favourably impressed; perhaps because I had lasted well and they didn't have to fiddle the results or give too much credit for the expanded tolerances allowed against age and experience. At the end, all his complaints seemed to come together on my inability to touch my toes without bending my knees. I could see it all slipping away on this one point; perhaps not important if I was to wear a kilt, but somehow vital for the flying of aeroplanes. It is better not to venture an opinion in medical matters, but I had not yet learned that, and so I expressed the opinion that this would be of little account when strapped in a cockpit. This seemed to increase his displeasure and he went over his figures and measurements again. At length, he declared himself: I was muscle-bound, but he entered up the vital column on his form, 'Fit A1'. This remark, when related to my workmates and companions, caused a good deal of hilarity at my expense. Misunderstanding the term, they were highly amused. These were men to whom strength was important. Their work demanded it and they developed a great strength and endurance, the ability to expend great effort over prolonged periods. This didn't show itself in their appearance, as it does in the professional muscle men, but they could demonstrate it by lifting a bag of corn in a straight unassisted lift off the barn floor, turning it as they lifted, to place it on their back and walk away without staggering or weaving, to deposit it easily on the cart. If required, they could do that all. The real heavies could do it with bags of barley. I was never in any danger of getting in that category but, nevertheless, I was as fit as a flea and medicals have never held any terror for me since.

The next stage was a two-day attestation or selection procedure, held in Edinburgh. Time seemed of little account to the RAF recruiter, or so it seemed to me then. Because of the timing, and in fairness to my employer, I had to quit my job so that they could hire another to start the new term. So this time, the days off were no problem, it was accepted that I was going to join the RAF. I tried to explain that I still had exams ahead and didn't rate my chances very high, but this was brushed aside. I had been a clever loon at school and everybody knew I could pass exams, and besides, there was a war on and they needed pilots.

And so the day dawned and some of my friends saw me off from Aberdeen station with a tot of warm whisky and some heavy-handed humour. 'Be sure to notice in Edinburgh that the main street had just one side', they said, 'and ask when they were to finish it'.

This was my first train journey of any length. Ever since, I have found nothing as exciting as the prospect of a journey, and particularly a train journey, which has a special magic of its own. The fact that it is usually tiring and dirty, often uncomfortable and crowded is irrelevant. One travels ever hopefully.

And so, on this first major trip, and I still see it as such, I looked about me at my travelling companions. It dawned on me that many of them were on the same ploy as myself and I was anxious to strike up their acquaintance. I was a little put off by their smart appearance and apparent sophistication. What was especially daunting was their knowledge of aviation matters and, in particular, their knowledge of what was to happen in Edinburgh, coupled with the scrolls they carried. These formidable documents turned out to be certificates of education of various sorts, heavily embossed with red seals and wrapped with ribbons.

I sat back soberly to assess my chances, that now somehow seemed very slim indeed. Yet I determined to give it a crack, give it all I had and, by golly, I would endeavour to enjoy it also.

The selection of aircrew is regarded as a serious business. In wartime, no doubt, it depends upon the urgency of the situation and the qualification standards are adapted to the circumstances. I decided to look around for a kindred spirit among my companions. I had a free ticket for Edinburgh, free accommodation at the YMCA, outside the window the countryside flew by, the telegraph lines dipped and rose like swallows in flight and an exciting prospect lay ahead.

At this distance in time a lot of the detail has faded. I recall two days of tests of various kinds, some whose purpose was evident, others not. There was a good deal of waiting about between events, and the medical, which fell on the second day, confirmed that. There were written tests that demanded a knowledge of current affairs, at that time mostly military affairs, the importance to Britain of the Channel ports and the like. I waded into those. At school, I had always liked writing essays and here, perhaps, was a chance to shine. I was also pretty well versed in military matters, thanks to Mrs Garden.

Mrs Garden was a small, frail lady who held court in her wooden sweet shop set in the corner of a field beside the turnpike at Culsalmond.[1] The youth of the district gathered there of an evening to refresh themselves from bottles of Hay's fizzy ale and Dazzle, with sweeties and even cigarettes, and to clown around as young people will. Mrs Garden was handicapped by the early onset of arthritis and struggled to make a living from her croft and roadside shop, and so raise her family. She was indomitable. Her belief that the British were winning the war was unshakeable. Although news of setbacks and defeats were then almost daily events, Mrs Garden defiantly set them aside, not by ignoring them, but by spirited explanations and defence. I took a less optimistic view and engaged her in argument, often playing the devil's advocate and, occasionally, was only bested when the good lady adapted her crutch from a means of support, to a weapon of defence.

It was on just such matters that the Air Force desired to hear my views and the views I expressed that day took on more of Mrs Garden's position than my own. I don't think I ever told her so, and now it's too late: the shop and the croft are long vanished and the corner of the field where they stood is, to all outward appearance, just another corner of just another field. There are places my mother will not visit because she says, they are peopled by ghosts. Up there, beside the turnpike, there is for me, just such a place.

Edinburgh itself was no disappointment. Prince's Street was magnificent. The Scots, I have often thought, have little enough

---

1 Culsamond, or Culsalmond, a parish in the district of Garioch, county of Aberdeen, two and a half miles north-west from Old Rayne.

to be proud of; little enough, when you think of all that pride, but Prince's Street is something to be proud of. No wonder Aberdonian friends made mock of it.

I had not managed to find a kindred spirit. We all seemed engrossed with our own affairs; indeed, there might even have been a spirit of competition among us. I noticed, somewhere, a dance advertised; probably on the notice board at the YMCA, and so I thought I might take a look at the local talent. The evening was a distinct failure. The local talent took, in turn, a look at me and we made no progress beyond comments on the band, or some such pleasantries.

The final stage of acceptance was an appearance before the board. The fierce and very senior officer, who was clearly the chairman, was in fact, very kindly. I think he liked the look of me and the others were ready to be influenced by him; a tendency of selection boards that I have noticed since then. I had failed in one subject, maths, and was to be given another shot at it. I could hardly believe my luck. No sense of foreboding or fears for the future intruded upon my delight.

In my part of Scotland, the worst thing you can be is 'bigsy': that is, to 'blaw' or boast about what you have done. If I had failed to make contact with my travelling companions on the way down, I certainly did nothing to endear myself to them on the return, as blaw I did, or at least enquire over-diligently after their scrolls. 'Were the board not impressed by them', I asked. 'Where were they?' Too precious to be put away inside a case on the way down, they seemed to have vanished from sight. Those of us who had been accepted tended then to congregate to talk of deferment and once again, they seemed to know about such things that were all new to me.

The next hurdle was maths. I'd had little occasion to use maths since leaving school, except perhaps to count my wages, and that didn't require higher maths. The test, in fact, had taken me beyond the maths I had covered at school and it was here that I had to come up to standard.

The Department of Education for Scotland, or whatever its title was then, wrote offering assistance by night school, or full-time day studies, but all of course, in far-off Aberdeen. The difficulty was solved by the dominie, Mr Grant. As I still had to support myself though I was living at home, and travel costs and lodging put Aberdeen outside my range, his solution was to take charge of the arrangements, seat me at the back of his class and provide whatever tuition I required during the intervals of school lessons, or at whatever natural breaks occurred. The Scots dominie is more than just a school headmaster, and Mr Grant was one of the old breed. Within their domain they were men of considerable importance and influence, which extended far beyond their school duties. I was most fortunate. The children, after the initial reaction, settled, just as he had said they would, accepting my presence there at the back of the class as if it was perfectly natural. I was the only one feeling uneasy about it. My family and friends accepted it almost as naturally, so any fears I had about it soon vanished.

The outcome was no longer in doubt and, when it ended with the retake of the exam again conducted by Mr Grant, my departure was tinged with regret as I was beginning to understand and enjoy my studies.

When John Shand, the roadman, heard I had passed, he settled back more comfortably on his shovel, took the pipe out of his mouth and pronounced upon the matter: 'You can send a donkey round the world and when it comes back to you, it's still a donkey'. Then he put away his pipe and, taking up his shovel, went back to work on the strip of roadside he had set as his stint for the day.

The traveller from Insch reacted to my success differently. He travelled the countryside on his bicycle, not exactly peddling his company's wares, but bringing his samples round the various districts for the ladies to choose from. From the carrier of his bike he lifted out his travelling case, neatly wrapped in its waterproof covering and firmly secured by leather straps. Assured of a welcome he would arrive on the doorstep (either the front or the back, depending upon his relationship with the householder) and ring at the bell or chap on the door. Once admitted inside, he laid away his case as inconspicuously as possible, and settled down to make serious enquiries about the welfare of the family. His memory was encyclopaedic, as was his knowledge of the countryside. Sooner or later, he could sense that the lady of the household was getting anxious to see the contents of his case. She had taken off her apron and cleared away the table, as often as not laying a clean cloth over it, or if the household didn't run to such niceties, wiping down the wax cloth. And then came the great moment, as, with his audience's anticipation rising, he carefully undid the straps, folded and put aside the covering and then without any great flourish, but with the sure knowledge of the salesman, began to display his wares.

Everything was of good quality but nothing was highly praised. He had a new line of this or that, but first he needed to know if the last had been satisfactory. He had been very pleased to learn just recently, that Mrs Middler (or whoever), had expressed her satisfaction with the ones she had bought. Then, as now, it often appeared that they weren't making things as well as they had in the past. But he would value your opinion if you'd like to try them. No mention was made of buying them and everything was clearly priced if you were bold enough to look. He was totally unaffected whether or not he made a sale and, if it was only a very small one, nothing more than a token purchase, it received the same dignified treatment that he would have accorded a large and valuable transaction. With the item entered up in his book and the arrangements completed, he would, just as carefully, fold away this treasure trove, keeping still to his business. Although the term 'impulse buying' had not been invented, he knew the notion well enough and, sometimes, if he knew the householder could afford it, he would leave out some small item, 'Just to save carrying it all back to Insch', he would say, and thus clinch a deal. But if he knew the household could not afford to order anything, the left-out item would genuinely be left lying there, with the same excuse, that he was getting on, you know, and the bag getting heavy, and, likely, there would be a new line in by the next time he called. The bag was carefully closed, wrapped and strapped up again. He would then settle down for a few minutes and continue the conversation about the family, filled and lit his pipe leisurely and calmly, and the room filled with the fragrance of his tobacco. Once it was well lit, he would make his departure and take the road.

On this occasion, I gather, it ended differently. My mother had a good sense of timing and, keeping the best till last, she told him her little piece of news. Her son was off to the RAF to be a pilot. He was incredulous. My mother thought he came close to suggesting that the laddie was lying, or at least, exaggerating a good bit. Anyway, I'm glad to say that their friendship survived and, thereafter, he never failed to enquire after my welfare and when I passed the various stages of training he was as delighted as she was. I learned later that she would read him bits from my letters now and again and, maybe if I'd known that, I would have been tempted to play to the gallery a little more.

Just as he would not wax fulsome about the quality of his wares, I would not wish to embarrass him by saying what a fine man he was and what a good friend he was to my family. But I would like to say that I was aware, while watching him open his Pandora's box, that I was watching a master craftsman at his trade.

The harsh business of having to earn a living again intruded on my life as the call to arms continued to be deferred. Here I made another useful discovery. Pay rates are better for casual labourers, the work is more interesting and varied and many advantages accrue. Combined with this, all the free time, living at home for the most part, and the feeling of freedom of being one's own man more than offset any anxiety about the next pay packet. The Local Defence Volunteers (later the Home Guard) provided some diversion for, although we laugh at them now, particularly in the television series *Dad's Army*. We were never, fortunately, put to the test.

There was one aspect of the LDV which should not be overlooked. Foremost among our supporters was the laird. It must

The author joined the Local Defence Volunteers, which became the Home Guard, while waiting to begin RAF training.

have given him a qualm to see this gang of would-be poachers turned guards, drilling in the school playground at Rothie. In this guise, armed with our shotguns and issued with ball cartridge, we had the run of the countryside. If ever we were issued with rifles and were able to use them, there might not be a deer left. Ammunition is difficult to account for, no matter how stringently controlled, as practice is needed and ammunition is easily lost. He need not have been concerned, we were unlikely to risk offending our chief supporter. It was the neighbouring landowners who had cause for concern.

Now, I was nearly ready to take the road. Some wag once said that the only high road the Scots ever take is the road to England. I can't leave the North-East with such a brief impression. One or two characters have appeared in my tale and have called to my mind a host of others to whom some acknowledgement is due, because the part they played went on to influence later events.

We see the world through eyes that evolution had positioned facing forward so that our vision fans out and the world we see centres upon ourselves. The place where the optic nerve is connected to the retina is a blind spot. This passes unnoticed as incessant small movements of the eye continuously shift the position of the image on the retina and, having two eyes, the part of the image that falls upon the blind spot of one eye is seen by the other. But this is not the only blind spot we have.

Within our mind's eye we see ourselves, perhaps in a different way from that physical appearance seen by others. The voice we hear within the bone dome of our skull is not necessarily the voice that the rest of the world hears. The first time you hear your voice recorded on tape may come as something of a shock. The deficiencies of the recording machine account for only a small part of the difference between what you expected to hear and what you do.

The impressions and habits of early life may be modified and discarded later, but nevertheless, they are the most deeply ingrained and late in life it is to these that we are likely to return. My daughter Helen noticed this early on. In later years, we annually packed ourselves inside a motor car and set off on the long, tedious drive, the length of the country to Scotland and Granny's. We were plagued by her question, 'How far is it now?' Only recently, Helen revealed that she always knew when we were getting close. 'Whenever we stopped for petrol, or whatever', she said, 'Dad's accent would change and puzzle me, and when he became well nigh incomprehensible, we were nearly there'.

Those closest to us and therefore most likely to make the most profound impression are our parents. This is most certainly true of my father and no less of my mother, but perhaps at two or three removes. My mother's brother, Charles Jaffrey, left for New Zealand shortly before I was born. He had emigrated there before the First World War but returned with the Anzacs. Having survived the blood-letting, he decided to give the old country one more go and took his demob in Britain. A blacksmith to trade, he came to regret his decision and quietly began to save his money for the cheapest one-way steerage back to the Antipodes. My mother recalls that he appeared one day in the harvest field where she was forking sheaves from the stooks on to the farm cart, and he took the pitchfork from her. Being heavy with child she was glad of the respite. He forked several loads, then kissed her and said goodbye. He was off, he said, but gave no indication as to where. She watched him stride away across the stubble, following his receding figure till he was long out of sight. She fancied that she could see the sunlight glinting on his yellow hair, although her sight was blurred by tears. Some premonition came upon her that she might never see him again. She decided, if her unborn child was a boy, that he would be named Charles Jaffrey.

My uncle worked his way south taking whatever jobs were offered to sustain himself, and arrived in good time to embark for Auckland. Among the passengers, indeed chief among them, was a new governor, outbound to take up his appointment. He may have been one of the Ferguson clan. At some point during the voyage, the new governor summoned all those who had been to New Zealand before to his cabin. He questioned my uncle closely when he heard his story.

Jeff had no fears about his arrival. His friend Jimmy Burr would likely be there to meet him and, with any luck, would have a job for him also, if only in unloading the ship. A day or two before they were due to dock, the governor sent for him again. He drew a wallet from his pocket and counted out in front of a very surprised Charles Jaffrey the sum of forty odd pounds, the exact cost of his fare.

With a fresh start such as this, one might suppose that he would have gone on to fame and fortune. Well, if not fame, at least to fortune. The trouble, he told me, was the twin handicap of slow horses and fast women. Apparently, his friend Jimmy was there at the quayside to meet him. Being as good as his word, he had a job waiting. They helped unload the ship. When that was done, they slaked their thirst and celebrated the wanderer's return and the unlooked-for improvement in his financial affairs. Having disposed of that, they set off inland.

They lie together now, the old comrades-in-arms, separated only by the pathway which divides the military cemetery at Pukekohe in south Auckland. Under the brilliant, clear light of those antipodean skies you fancy that you could reach out and touch the Bombay Hills, which mark the horizon, so near do they appear to be. It would be hard to imagine a more beautiful spot to lie at rest, or better companions to share it with.

My father was struck down early in life by a cruel misfortune that left him paralysed down his left side. The family rallied round with practical help and my grandparents took us all in. The state, in those days, did not accept responsibility for the welfare of its citizen. It is no small tribute to the way my parents coped that their children barely knew that something dreadful had happened. Indeed, the idea of staying with our maternal grandparents seemed highly desirable.

My father set about the slow business of recovery, from being an invalid right through to being a man with something of a handicap, but able to earn a living again. If he'd had a physiotherapist, he or she would have been pleased with and proud of him. Somewhere along the way, it changed the kind of man he was. The struggle, first for survival and then to improve his physical ability, brought out qualities that might otherwise never have emerged. He generally was able to look on the bright side: not to reject blindly these ugly circumstance but to find some hopeful aspect of his life.

Nothing attracts people so much as the sound of laughter and merriment, and this was true of my father. He drew to him people who liked laughter or needed to hear it. Chief among these was my Auntie Lizzie. Laughter seemed to be part of her, it bubbled from her like champagne released from the bottle, she frothed and sparkled. When she and my father were together at a Sunday family dinner, this laughter was a catalyst after the great hullabaloo of greeting, then a quiet little while of verbal sparring and then it would begin, and we were all caught up in it. I hear the echoes still.

We children ran about filled with a great excitement, Eddie Cassie arrived full of worries and grouses, my father saying, 'Eddie has gone to a growl'. There he would be, leaning back in one of the sturdy chairs my grandfather had made, putting every tenon joint at risk, and holding his sides because they hurt. Mr Parker, the grieve, not a man given to unseemly behaviour, would be shaking like a great tree in the wind, his face hidden behind a work-roughened hand. John Emslie's voice would rise above the rest, rivalled only by that of Aunt Elsie. My grandmother would come through from within the house, well ahead of her usual time and sit quietly amidst the din like somebody come into sit by a roaring fire and warming themselves at it with deep appreciation. My mother rushed about, anxious for the dinner, distracted by the need to listen out for the children which put the tatties in grave danger of either being hard in the middle or turning to soup in an instant.

Some while before Auntie Lizzie went to Canada to visit her daughter, they found her all packed and dressed and waiting in the lobby ready for the off. Thinking she was getting confused, they asked her why. She said she was waiting for Charlie, who would be along presently to take her to Canada. Dear Aunt Lizzie, I don't think your mind was wandering, I was the one who had it wrong and failed to keep the tryst. In any list of VIPs of heads of state or well-known people whom I have transported, you would have been at its head.

As my father progressed, taking on gardening and other odd jobs, it became clear that his range of employment was limited for lack of transport. So one day a tricycle appeared. I don't know how it got there but it had cost a great deal of money. It was a heavy black brute of a machine and unknown to us its designer had built into it a fearful instability. Somewhere in between the start of roll and its cruising speed it became well-nigh uncontrollable. At this critical stage, if not firmly restrained, it would turn sharply towards the ditch, causing the rider to fall headlong into the road. It would wind up with the front wheel athwart ship and any damage done to it was due more to the rider's sudden departure then anything else. My father was determined to master it and when his progress became uneven this was no occasion for laughter. Master it he did and he became a familiar figure in the district, pedalling away at a steady pace, very often with his gardening tools strapped to the frame, for which purpose the machine seemed well adapted.

Of course, it caused a good deal of comment and interest. Children would run after him and, even adults, who should have known better, shouted at him as he passed. Nothing pleased him better than to have a group of youths shouting out at him.

On would go the brake and the contraption juddered to a halt. He dismounted carefully and, if the group had not run away at this juncture, he would turn the machine around and push it towards them. Selecting the ringleader, he would challenge him to ride it. The youth could hardly do otherwise without loss of face. Whether he attempted to mount it as you would an ordinary cycle, or boarded it from the rear, having watched my father dismount, he would come to grief. My father would pretend to give him a hand, but what he really did was to give him a great shove to get him started. The trike then reached its most dangerous speed before the unwary youth had got the hang of it and off he came, to land painfully in the road. My father would go on his way in great good humour and, if they shouted at him again, it was in quite another spirit.

But others were also interested by this strange sight. Here and there, the farm dogs, their day's work over, were keeping an eye out for passing traffic and generally lying in wait for strangers at the gate. They were not readily discouraged. One old collie that lived at the foot of the hill persisted when the others had all tired of the game. My father had to make special arrangements for him. At the foot of the hill, before he reached the end of the farm road, he would brake to a halt and dismount. He then walked over to the hedge and reached in for his stick, carefully plonked there from the last passage. Then risking life and limb, grasping the stick and the handle bar together in his right hand, he cranked up speed aided by the slight downhill. Every move was watched by unseen eyes. Choosing its moment carefully, the dog rushed out barking furiously, and my father, casting discretion to the winds, lashed out with the stick. The dog contrived to stay just out of range. Once safely past, my father dismounted again, put the stick back into its other hiding place and proceeded on his way. The dog disappeared from sight and, with infinite patience, awaited his return. I would be hard put to it to say who enjoyed the contest more.

Keeping the tricycle serviceable was a problem. No one claimed it and no maker's name adorned it. Letters went off to the Midlands seeking spare parts from the better known cycle makers of the day. The saddler in Insch was a dab hand with cycles but leather and fabrics were his forte. He looked disapprovingly at the tricycle.

The blacksmith had his premises at the crossroads and once he had done one or two repairs to the trike, he took it as a challenge. There was nothing made of metal that he would not repair or duplicate or modify. If parts were not forthcoming, parts could be made or standard bicycle fittings adapted. Although he might be busy with the harvest starting and farmers arriving with broken machines from all over the district, left broken, usually from last year's harvest, he would put down his tools and survey the trike brought for his attention. 'The farmers will be howling for their binders', said my father. 'Let them howl', the blacksmith would say without looking up, for a machine like that needed all his concentration.

When the tricycle was no longer needed my mother sold it. It had been a source of worry and expense and no one rushed to buy it. Such things were no longer in demand. She begrudged letting it go for next to nothing. I thought, privately, that it had more than earned its keep, but I didn't say so: some things are best left unsaid. I'll have to tread warily. Things seen through the eyes of a child are not the things the adult sees. If ever my mother reads any of this, a good deal of it will be called up for revision.

Jamie Duff was also not one to be forgotten. The Duffs took over Gammies' old shop in Newseat, Country shops are always something of an emporium and, so it was with Jamie, who would trade in anything likely to show a return. My father found employment there as handyman and general factotum. He and Jamie Duff went beyond any employer/employee relationship I have ever seen and were more like cronies. The very last thing anyone noticed about Jamie was that he was a cripple. Today we would call him an entrepreneur. There were a good many such shops and their vans covered the district, competing with each other for trade. Jamie did a thriving business, not because his goods were better or his schedule reliable, but because folk liked him. Money was short and customers hard to please. They needed to be jollied along and entertained or their custom went elsewhere. It was something of a two-way trade. The country wives relied on selling their eggs and other produce to pay the household expenses and were sometimes not above a little sharp practice. If hens strayed and laid away, a dozen or so dubious eggs might be found in a nest beside the straw ricks and then find their way in among the others. Jamie Duff could tell a bad egg from a good better than most, but never a word was said. There were other times to think of; the time when the hens were up for sale before Christmas and had to be brought in to be plucked and packed for the markets in the south. In wintry weather, when the other vans were stormbound, Jamie enjoyed nothing more than turning out for the rounds, the van wheels chained and my father with him in the cab, a well-oiled snow shovel between them. There was no saying when or in what condition they might return.

Many a country housewife, long abed against the cold, snowed in at the far end of a farm road, having reconciled herself to whatever provisions she had already made with the oatmeal girnel[2] and the salt fish hanging in the cellar, would wake to hear the toot of the van arriving much later than its time. She could hardly stay there but would have to turn out, grumbling maybe the while, but not for long when the two billies arrived.

They went to roups,[3] as Jamie had an eye for a good piece of furniture and couldn't resist a competition anyway. During the sale, my father found employment holding up the items at the auctioneer's behest and, if James Duff was among the bidders, it was often wise to let him win and drop out. The auctioneers liked this, as they too had to warm up their audience and a little good-natured badinage helped. The rubbishy lots at the end often got knocked down to J Duff. After the sale, my father had to pack it all into the van. By then, Jamie was involved in more serious negotiations to cover his expenses as

2 A meal chest or barrel.

3 Auctions or sales.

disappointed bidders chanced a few extra shillings to secure the item they had set their heart on.

There was another sort of competition that Jamie sponsored. The postie, a great bellowing bull of a man, put together a tug-of-war team. They would often be seen practising for the summer shows and Highland Games outside Gammies' shop. They tied a great iron spring device to a tree and laid themselves along the rope. If it attracted enough bystanders, they would be cajoled to join together to give the team a tug.

Numbers were no object, and the more the merrier, as many as could get hold of the rope, could enter. It was thirsty work and good for trade, but the intention was serious. The postie was a man of ideas and boundless enthusiasm. He devised and taught his team a set of tactics. By the standards of the day they were little more than lightweights. Compared with the great heavyweight teams fielded by the Glasgow police, or the Bell family, they looked insignificant. But they had a hold whereby they laid on the rope, determined not to be shifted to wear down and tire their opponents. They had a check to stop the slide and to catch the others off balance. They had a rapid fire tug that, once started, was difficult to counter and they had the postie himself. His timing was impeccable, his appearance and behaviour arresting. The Wartle team became something to contend with. James Duff took a huge delight in them.

For me, however, it was a different matter. He had a great collection of gramophone records. Our old gramophone had seen better days but Jamie would loan me not only his records to play but his gramophone as well. The real musical treasures among these were the corn kisters. Now, in case these are not familiar to you, I had best explain.

In the farm stables, the horses were fed and bedded by six o'clock. The horsemen then trooped off to the farm kitchen for their supper. That over, they repaired to the stable to while away the evening till nine o'clock and bedtime. In each window bay stood the corn chest or kist, holding the supply of oats. These formed a convenient seat for two or three with a place to tap your heels. The men told stories and they sang. The songs were ballads of bonny lassies, farm touns,[4] farm queans[5] and country affairs. These were corn kisters. 'Ah', you say, 'folk music'. In fact, these songs are a rich treasury for today's pedlars of 'folk'. They take the tune and turn it into a kind of dirge that suits a guitar. They take the words and anglicise them from the broad Scots dialect of the district. To my mind, they are ruined, the humour and the pathos lost. A form of vandalism. Not always of course, nothing is ever all loss. Did you notice, perhaps, that when the pipers of Montgomery's Eighth Army led the march into Tripoli in that famous victory, the pipe tune was *The Mucking of Geordie's Byre*? There's a corn kister for you, and how sweetly was it adapted for the occasion.

Jamie Duff was a great hand at corn kisters. He was the kind of man you'd like to sing and dance at your wedding. I'm pleased to say he did so at mine.

Watching over his parish the Reverend Donald Cameron knew more about his parishioners than they sometimes wished for their own comfort. To a boy he was an imposing and slightly terrifying figure. I learnt afterwards that not only did boys go in some awe of him. If misdeeds came to his notice there was no guarantee that such wrongdoing might not be aired in public from the pulpit. For a good many, that might have held more terror than hell-fire to come. But he was ready with praise and encouragement for his Sunday school class, if they learnt their catechism. To earn a good word from him was a rich reward. Once I acquired a bicycle. Not a new one you understand, but new to me and in lovely condition, if perhaps a bit too big. As I cycled along, I noticed a tall black figure approaching round a bend in the road. It was too late to take another direction or turn back. I pedalled onwards. As I came up to him, I jumped off and waited his approach. It is sometimes best to get the first word on. 'Here's my new bike', I said. 'What do you think of my

---

4 Small settlements, or fermtouns, of up to twenty households growing their food on surrounding strips of common land.

5 A woman, almost always a young, unmarried one, a lass, a girl.

new bike?' He stopped and looked. 'It's bonny', he admitted, then as he resumed his progress he called out, 'All things are bonny when they're new.'

The author with a Boeing Stearman.

Needle, ball and airspeed

One September day in 1941 I set off for Lord's Cricket Ground. A fitting place to start from, I thought, perhaps with a game of cricket in the English tradition. Drake and his bowls came to mind. I wondered what they'd make of my version of their national game. At Rayne school we had only one bat and one wicket and we played without sides or niceties such as overs. With one bowler and one batsman, the others all fielded. Since I had no eye for a ball, my tenure as batsman was generally short lived. As a fielder I was, if anything, worse, and could be relied upon to muff any catch that came my way. I had, perforce, to acquire some merit as a bowler to keep out of trouble.

As I travelled south, I glanced with pride at my Uncle Jamie's leather case, which contained the few things I had brought, and I looked forward to meeting my first Englishman when we reached Newcastle. The train pulled in for its scheduled ten-minute stop and the compartment rapidly filled up with a lively party intent on making a noisy and boisterous farewell. I listened closely, and although enjoying its evident good humour and spirit, I was dismayed by the accent. It sounded altogether like a foreign language. One of the group addressed me directly. 'What's the time hinny?' he cried. I was floored. He pointed to my wristwatch, and so, comprehending at last, I gave answer. He didn't appear to understand my reply for he grabbed my wrist to look for himself. There was time for a cup of tea apparently, and we set out together to find one at his insistence. I was loath to leave the train. What if it left without us, and what of Uncle Jamie's case? Tea was followed by the offer of something stronger to lace it, and so I was caught up with my travelling companions. Everything I had ever heard seemed to contradict this experience. I had understood that the English preferred to travel together in frigid silence, and I was unprepared for the reality. I was soon given to understand that these were Geordies – Geordies first and Englishmen second. I began to get the hang of their accent, although the same could not be said of mine and we rattled along through the night in cheerful company. Gradually as sleep took its toll, I relaxed, warmed by the thought that I should have no difficulty among such people and that, with a little modification to my broad Scots, I could make myself better understood. I have had a warm spot for the Geordies ever since.

I don't remember much of the Lords Cricket Ground, except that it seemed strangely gaunt and empty, an unlikely setting for schoolboy heroes and the home of so much tradition. St Johns Wood was our immediate destination. There we began our indoctrination and were kitted out as airmen and aircrew cadets. As is customary with reception centres, waiting is the major occupation, interspersed with marching to the Regents Park Zoo at feeding times (our feeding times, not the animals). Then there were visits to the uniform stores to be kitted out. There must have been a rush on some items for, although there seemed an unlimited supply of webbing harness and water bottles, the uniform department had got down to a strange selection of ill-fitting garments. Standard sizes did not appear to be in stock. We were assured that at the back, however, there was an army of tailors and seamstresses who could adapt the most unlikely garment to fit. A little letting out or taking in here and there and all would be well. I was left with a lasting suspicion of the tailoring trade, since reinforced by various bespoke tailors in places like Singapore and Hong Kong.

In all of this there was plenty of time to investigate the capital itself, particularly by Underground railway, which offered a dazzling variety of well-known places to be visited. We would pop up like rabbits from such underground bolt holes. I don't quite know why, but I found the place disappointing and soon tired of it. I was uneasily aware of Dr Johnson's dictum, 'A man who is tired of London is tired of life.' Under the circumstances, perhaps London wasn't at its best. I have never acquired a liking for London. At the time, I found it too expensive and in that respect, it doesn't seem to have changed.

Among the ranks of my fellow recruits, I made one or two friends. One was another Scots lad from Dundee. Alick was a musician. Perhaps to be more precise, he played the bagpipes. After a deal of consideration, he had decided not to bring them along. Although they were reasonably portable, he had felt they might not fit into a kitbag along with whatever other clobber we would have to carry, and practising might be a problem. I think he regretted his decision but, as his mother had been insistent that he continue to practise, he had done the next best thing and brought his chanter. At first he was shy of producing it, but suitably encouraged, he was prevailed upon to give us a tune. At this time the Scots lads had naturally tended to congregate and the chanter did nothing to make us popular. However, I'm sure his mother would have been pleased as, once he started, practise he did, whatever the circumstances.

The author in the uniform of an RAF trainee pilot.

We shortly set out for our initial training, split up into groups and posted to initial training wings throughout the country. I had the good fortune to be sent to the unit at Babbacombe, near

Torquay. From the stripped-down luxury flats of St Johns Wood, we repaired to the equally bare boards of the luxury hotels and guest houses in this delightful seaside resort. The waiting was over with a vengeance as we were initiated into the diverse arts of military aviation. In case all the sitting around in classrooms was bad for us, the physical training instructors weighed in heavily with their programmes of exercises and drill. Such hardy holidaymakers or visitors who had managed to escape the vicissitudes of war and who were up and about early might well have been entertained to see our awkward squads along the cliff tops and pleasure gardens, accompanied by PT corporals who loudly lamented our lack of physical fitness and our un-airman-like appearance.

The classroom work was at once interesting and daunting, in that it was soon apparent that there was a great deal to learn and to start with we were only scratching the surface. The theory of flight and navigation is a hard slog if removed too far from practical work in airfields and aeroplanes. But I didn't have long to wait for my introduction to both. By this time it was clear that the skies over Britain were too crowded for training and a programme of training overseas had got underway. Before the cadet was allowed to take up a space on a troopship, his aptitude was tested in a grading course. There is no better aptitude test than sitting in a little aeroplane and learning to fly it. Somewhere near Peterborough, I made my first flight in a Tiger Moth. The winter weather made the flying spasmodic, however, my instructor seemed satisfied with my progress. But at the time I was ready to fly solo, the airfield was blanketed in snow and I had to forego this reward.

Thereafter, my progress through the training was unremarkable, although not without incident. The story has been duplicated ten thousand times and more. Perhaps the only thing unusual about mine was that I was sent to the United States for flying training, having survived the grading school assessment.

Number One British Flying Training School was a strange blend of civil and military international cooperation. The

Like tens of thousands of other cadets, the author learnt to fly at the controls of a de Havilland Tiger Moth.

United States Army Air Corps furnished the equipment right down to the uniforms we wore. All we retained of our RAF garb was the forage cap. The instructors were civilian, a great bunch of guys who seemed to have no difficulty whatever in working with foreign military cadets. The local people knew us as the British boys and, to them, we were neither foreign nor military. In Terrell we were their boys.

One solitary officer, Mr Palmer, represented the RAF, acting as liaison man between the separate groups. Although we were all very young and rather raw and green, we were most fortunate to have this urbane and suave ambassador to represent us. Mr Palmer straightened out any problem or difficulty that might arise. The townspeople liked and admired him. When cadets got into trouble, usually over girls, Mr Palmer smoothed things over. When two aeroplanes collided and the cadets were killed, Mr Palmer arranged the funeral with due military honours and allayed anxiety all round. Lord Halifax, an important diplomat and politician at that time, came from Washington to attend and address the funeral. This was a sad episode, perhaps a foretaste of what was to come and, it cast a brief shadow over us. Equally quickly, we had to put it behind us and the flying training proceeded apace in the clear skies over Texas.

I learnt a good many things from the Texans. The most lasting of these was that I shared their love of freedom and independence. Of more immediate and just as lasting value was their ability to fly on instruments. Scanning the panel was taught by reiterating, 'needle, ball and airspeed'. To watch a skilled instrument pilot is always a joy. 'The dials rotate, but the needles are stuck to the glass', was how Wally Macfarlane put it.

In Texas, the author progressed to the Boeing Stearman biplane.

My first instructor was a man called Mitchell. Under his able tuition I made steady progress. We were allotted alphabetically, three students to an instructor, for the basic course on the old Stearman biplanes. The Stearman was a more robust version of the RAF's Tiger Moth and just as much fun to fly and I soon ran into the problem of over-confidence which besets the new pilot.

I set off one day on a straightforward solo cross-country flight. Nothing could have been simpler, and I fell to daydreaming. On the last leg home, I realised that I was lost or, at least, uncertain of my position. The landmarks I was looking for failed to appear and the ones that did, couldn't be fitted to the map. I cursed myself for a fool. I decided on a precautionary landing and cast about for a suitable field. Presently I spotted what looked nearly ideal, a good-sized field alongside a farmhouse. I did it all as I'd been taught: it was one of Mr Mitchell's favourite party pieces. Seeing me engrossed on some manoeuvre, he would cut the motor and leave me to sort out the wind direction, select a suitable field and position for a forced landing. He also taught me to differentiate between a forced landing and a precautionary one. So I ran through the drill, making a low-level pass to check the surface of the field and, when satisfied that all was in order, I motored in for the landing. It wasn't as smooth as it had looked from the air, but it served well enough and I came to a stop and cut off the engine, not without some hesitation, in case I should have to restart it.

Presently, the farmer appeared from the vicinity of the farmhouse to check on his unexpected visitor. I expected something of a drama, but no; he treated me as if it were the most natural thing in the world for a passing aviator to drop by and quickly set me to rights. I tried to make things better by adding that I'd got low on gas. Gas was no problem, he had plenty of gas. I looked at his battered farm truck and briefly wondered about octane ratings and the like. I was sorry I'd mentioned it. I decided to stick with the procedures. Had he got a telephone? I'd best call my base. This puzzled him a bit. 'Sure', he said, but clearly he didn't wholeheartedly approve; 'they'll only fuss', he said. He was right, they fussed. 'Hold everything', they said. A rescue truck was dispatched with an instructor to fly the aeroplane out and mechanics to check it over, and fuel and everything.

The farmer's wife decided that I must be hungry. Getting lost was hungry work and we filled the time till the rescue truck appeared. 'Be sure to call by again', said the farmer. I regret to say I never did. I survived the check flight with the chief flying instructor. Maybe my reports had been better than I thought. Getting washed out and sent off to Trenton was something we all dreaded.

We moved on from the Stearman and the basic course to the intermediate, a Vultee monoplane. This was a little more demanding and I remember it as an aeroplane that could not be taken for granted and was less forgiving of errors than the Stearman. Along with the change came a new instructor. I always think of him as one of a great breed of barnstormers, although in fact, this wasn't exactly the case. I remember he told me he was an ex-Navy man, and barnstorming was just one of the many things he'd done. He straightened me out on any problems I might have had with cross-countries and landing away. 'Take me into Love Field', he'd say. I'd find my way to Love Field, join the traffic pattern, land and taxi in. 'Get yourself a cup of coffee', he'd say, and disappear on some ploy of his own. 'Now get me the hell out of here', he'd say.

We did our night flying out of an auxiliary field under a beautiful Texas moon. I couldn't tell if he was still awake there behind me as I motored round the circuit. An occasional growl served to remind me he was. 'Don't drag it in across the fence, you'll bust your ass'. I corrected my approach path. I managed not to bust my ass.

At this stage, we were given leave, and permission to go anywhere within the USA. Almost without exception, the cadets headed for Hollywood. It was known by now that a great reception could be expected there from the British film star contingent. Nobby Clarke and I decided against the long haul to the West Coast. We both had a notion to see more of Texas and, if time permitted, maybe get as far as Mexico. We planned to hitch-hike, and also to meet the people. We wanted to see the King country of the cowboys, that home on the range of the Wizard and the Rover, and maybe the oil wells of Kilgore, and soak up the atmosphere and legend of the lone-star state.

With such an attitude we couldn't go wrong, Texas took us to her heart. We started out from Fort Worth, with its drugs tore cowboys and struck pay dirt at once.

A rancher and his wife were heading home when, on an impulse, they stopped to offer a ride to these two student boys, maybe a coupla kids from some military school. It took a while to set the record straight. When it got to their turn-off the rancher pulled over. We made our goodbyes and thanked them profusely, as is the British way. The rancher glanced at his wife. 'Maybe', he said, 'You-all mean that stuff about seeing Texas. We got a small spread just a mite from here, you'd be most welcome'. It was stupendous. They had three houses on the ranch to make it possible to work the place. They dressed us up in high-heeled boots and large hats and put us on horseback. They had never met anyone who couldn't ride and who insisted on falling off. Nobby and I enjoyed ourselves

The author relaxes on a Texas porch.

hugely. We had to tear ourselves away. 'You-all come back', they said. We made great progress towards the border. We proved that it is better to travel hopefully than to arrive. The Customs officials were very kind and let us cross into Mexico, but only for that day. Border towns are not very exciting and besides, it was time to head back. Leaving El Paso was easier said than done. The hitches were slow in coming. At this stage, our finances would have been stretched to run to paying for transport. We decided to split up on the basis that one can hitch-hike better than two, and planned to meet up in Dallas, or failing that, back at camp. I was to encounter quite another sort of Texan hospitality on the way. I made it as far as Waco and checked into a small hotel. I left my bag and set off down Main Street. I had surely got myself deep in the heart of Texas.

I passed a saloon. I couldn't resist the swing doors. I sat down at the bar and ordered a beer. I planned to eat if there was anywhere cheap enough, and hit the sack early. Just as I was finishing my beer and thinking of moving on, there was a sudden commotion. The swing doors burst open amidst the sound of voices shouting orders. I saw my fellow customers throw themselves to the floor, and the barman disappeared from sight. I don't suppose I thought of it until afterwards, but it was just like the enactment of any corny Hollywood western. I turned slowly towards the door, half expecting to see a gunslinger poised there ready for the shoot-out. The doorway was crowded with a curious mixture of police and quasi-military-looking men. The guns they held seemed real enough and they were pointed at me. Slowly, I started to raise my hands above my head.

Suddenly I was seized by the gunmen and bundled unceremoniously out of the door. They threw me into the back of a black maria. They crowded in behind me and we roared off at speed. I found myself in a prison cell with, what looked like armed wardens guarding me. I found out later that they were wardens from the local penitentiary. I also discovered that I had been mistaken for an escaped desperado who had chosen that day to go over the wall. For the time being, however, I had no idea what was going on and reflected sadly on the loss of my hotel room deposit. It was clear that I was to have accommodation at public expense in Waco jail. If I'd only known. My captors reacted sourly. Presently a senior figure appeared and with him the first niggling doubts arose. I produced my RAF identity card, my form twelve fifty. I was aware that had little authority under the circumstances, but every official-looking chitty carries some weight and it was enough to give him pause. By the time he got through to Terrell and talked to Mr Palmer, the Texan was a changed man. Then it seemed, they were as anxious to be rid of me as they had been to grab me in the first place. Ungracious to the end, they ran me out of town.

By this time I had got through the intermediate to the advanced class and the Harvards. I'm not given to any great affection for particular aeroplanes or, indeed machines of any kind, just as long as they are designed for and fit their purpose, but I liked the Harvard. I think, if such things are possible, that it liked me. And besides, I got my old instructor back again. I hadn't realised that the instructors flew anything and everything with equal facility.

Mitchell took the Harvard all apart for me again and reassembled it to his liking and I began to advance steadily to a pretty fair standard of flying, curbing any exuberance or dare-devil tendency and letting my natural caution rule. I probably reached a high point under Mitchell's tuition and managed to end on a high note.

Cruising back to Terrell one day, the reduction gear failed. This is the bit joining the engine to the propeller which, among other things, provides the gearing between the higher revving motor and the slower turning propeller. Obeying the natural forces upon it, the propeller ran into fine pitch and the engine revs mounted. As I hauled back on the throttle to contain the engine revs the oil from the reduction gear spread back, smearing the windscreens. I found, in this sequence of events, that I could keep the thing going, the reduced airspeed keeping the engine RPM within bounds and shedding height gently to

Jeff Gray enjoyed flying the Harvard: 'I think, if such things are possible, that it liked me.'

compensate for the reduction in power.

I dismissed the idea of a forced landing; mainly because of the smeared screens, and set about nursing the aeroplane home. I even managed a nice curved approach so that I could see the field on the way in, in what I imagined was the way the fighter boys did it with their long-nosed machines. I snagged the reduction gear and asked for the screen to be cleaned off, and remembering my farmer friend, generally downplayed the incident. I think I got it wrong again, but at least Mitchell was pleased when I told him and that, for me, was what counted.

The final exams loomed ahead, and here an element of farce crept in. We'd been following a ground school course along a basic US Army format, which had served the previous courses well enough. However, in faraway Washington the RAF chipped in with a set of examination papers derived from the basic RAF training. This posed a severe problem for the school, as we were to take an examination based upon a course we hadn't covered. Very sensibly, the school sought the help of the students to sort this out and, between us, from our old initial training wing stuff we were able to come up with the answers. Somewhat ungraciously, as is the manner of authority everywhere, they made us sit their own examinations as well.

Someone came from Washington to present our wings. We mostly already had them, carefully stitched on our blue RAF tunics. I was disappointed that we didn't receive the American Air Corps wings also, as did our counterparts who had trained under the official Arnold scheme. However, when I later compared notes with the boys who had been trained formally by the American Army, I didn't begrudge them this additional honour. I think they earned it!

Now, however, came a surprise. Six of us were offered instructors' posts with the Air Corps, including honorary rank and real pay. In retrospect, we like to think that our lives are somehow ordered following a defined pattern and making a piece, but here and there, things occur to show that this is not so. A decision, intentional or otherwise at some point can shift the pattern in ways which cannot be foreseen. Here was one such point, and I hardly gave it a moment's thought. The air war in Europe was far advanced and that was where I was headed, so I turned the offer down.

Thirty-six years later, I had occasion to revisit Texas, appointed by an airline to inspect flying schools for their national training programme. In the mind's eye, places and people are frozen in the image of that time, as in an old photograph album. You know that changes have occurred, but the mind cannot cope with the reality. The Dallas and Fort Worth I knew had changed beyond recognition and, though I stood on the tarmac at Love Field, it was as if the past had never existed. Had I ever waited here over a cup of coffee for Bartlett to reappear, ready to snap: 'Get me the hell out of here'?

It would be nice to record that I was able to award the contract to a Texan flying school, but it was not to be. The competing claims of a school in California were stronger than the nostalgia I felt for my beloved Texas.

There was some delay before I set off back to the UK. I took advantage of this to visit friends in Dallas and managed to overstay so I had to make my own way to Moncton. Fortunately no one noticed and I rejoined my colleagues awaiting embarkation. We came back on the *Andes*, one of the great British liners of the day. Although she was not as famous as the Queens, like them she sailed solo across the Atlantic, outrunning the U-boat packs. Stripped out and spartan in her role as troop ship, she somehow retained the grace and elegance of her line. We fed like fighting cocks and I enjoyed the trip. This journey was quite unlike our outboard voyage in convoy, crowded miserably in an old hulk rejoicing in the name *Banfora*, in which we had slogged our way across, cramped and miserable and ill-fed, and somehow very conscious of the dangers of sea travel at that time. On the *Banfora* we lived between decks, eating, sleeping and generally existing together. By night we slung hammocks from the ceiling and somehow contrived to get into them and stay in them. No one showed us how to do this, and we learnt by trial and error. If the hammocks were slung too low, for easy accessibility, your body protruded below the general mass of bodies, and suffered severe bumping and disturbance from those whose bladders were small or who otherwise became lively with nightfall when the majority succumbed to sleep.

By day, narrow tables and benches were rigged up, each capable of seating a dozen people in comparative comfort. On our voyage they each had to accommodate twenty. The galley was some way off. Two buckets were provided per table and we took it in turn to convey the food to the diners, one bucket for the main course and one for the pudding. These were not ordinary buckets and when I mentioned them to my wife, now turned typist, she recognised them immediately from her army nursing days. They were tall and narrow, fitted with a spout for pouring, a lid to protect the contents and a carrying handle. When you reached the front of the queue with your bucket the cook filled it up. In would go the Brussels sprouts, then perhaps, the potatoes and finally the pork chops, topped off with a dollop of apple sauce and gravy. Your companion with

The author returned to Britain aboard the liner RMS *Andes*. After the war she became a cruise ship and remained in service until 1971.

the sweet bucket, would similarly, have it filled with portions of steamed pudding and an ample supply of custard.

Then began the return along the deck, often swept by sea and wind, to the ladders. I am aware that they are not called ladders in nautical parlance, but that's what they were. You descended carefully, one hand occupied with the bucket, the other on the handrail, but any unexpected gyration of the ship would send a bucket flying, making life more hazardous for anyone following, and disappointing those waiting below who still had an appetite. The food had to be served up in reverse order, dependent upon the consistency of the mix, and if you were unlucky enough to be last, your dinner that day might consist of little more than Brussels sprouts.

On the *Andes* it seemed impossible that anything as mighty and proud as this ship could be threatened. The crew seemed to share that belief and treated us well, according us a respect for our sergeants' stripes and flying brevet which we had not earned and was, of course, quite novel. There is somehow a world of difference between sprog aircraftsmen and sergeant pilots, even if they are the same fellows but differently adorned and completely untried.

I volunteered for ship's duties. The chief purser explained what these were. The passengers, as he called them, had to eat in sittings. Regrettably, despite the generosity of the helpings, there were those who attempted to go round twice and this he had to discouraged. We were to act as dinner monitors. We were issued with arm bands bearing the legend SP. 'Curiouser and curiouser', said Alice. These badges somehow set us apart, gave us the run of the ship. Although we were merely sheep in wolves' clothing, I was uneasily aware that, however trivially, I had now sided with power. Not that there was any need to keep order, for from somewhere out of sight, came a sense of authority. The phrase, 'Running a tight ship', took on meaning.

Right at the end of the voyage there came a pleasant surprise. We were summoned to the purser's office. He opened a large cash box, called us forward one at a time and presented each of us with an ex gratia payment and a word of thanks for our efforts. This was doubly welcome to me in that it was completely unexpected, and it went a long way to make up my funds, so sadly depleted before my late return to Moncton.

I went ashore solvent. I left the *Andes* with regret and a new-found respect for the men who go down to the sea in ships. My first impression on my return to the UK was that the place had shrunk. The train we boarded was tiny and divided up into impossibly small compartments. When, it set off, we chugged our way past diminutive houses all crowded together and at length came to a landscape of tiny fields scattered about with dwarf trees. I wondered how long this Lilliputian effect would last. Mercifully, darkness fell and with it, the scale seemed to return to normal. To say that darkness fell is quite wrong. Darkness was already there, had pervaded the landscape and possessed it and merely thickened and intensified until all that was left of the world was a dimly lit, smoke-filled compartment, now racing, now clanking fitfully over an unseen track to an unknown destination.

The destination turned out to be Harrogate, a royal spa of immense Victorian dignity, and by the time we came arrived there, things had returned to their normal dimensions. The Grand Hotel had been stripped of its furniture and fittings for our stay, but, like the *Andes*, it had not been denuded of its grandeur and the gardens, though dank and bare in their winter grime, had been left untouched to await the spring. If the hotel had somehow survived the indignity of being turned into a military billet, the town itself had not noticed at all, and all this helped in a rapid transition back to the world of wartime Britain and the RAF.

The waiting began again and, with it, efforts to fill the time. A month in Whitley Bay with the PT corporals of the Royal Air Force Regiment provided a gloomy diversion, but clearly, the authorities wanted to chase away any lingering disposition in us towards independence in outlook and dress and had shepherded us back into the fold. The commando assault training must also have helped them to satisfy their mania for fitness among aircrew. The ability to touch one's toes was still held in great esteem in high places. We learnt to skive, to avoid the worst excesses of cross-country runs and drill parades. I enjoyed the assault course: leaping about over ditches and swinging on ropes is satisfying in itself.

Clearly there were worries also about the standard of our overseas training and deficiencies had to be made good. Before proceeding to the operational training unit (OTU), further fillers were devised. I remember only the simulated night flying. Units had been provided with the Airspeed Oxford, known affectionately as the Ox-Box, and sodium flare paths had been laid on the field. By fitting students with dark goggles and providing extra lighting in the cockpit, a fair simulation of a night flare path could be attained, and the student endeavoured to fly circuits and landings, enmeshed in all the clobber, with an ever-watchful and bad-tempered instructor alongside. It was hot work, and the goggles steamed up: everything steamed up, particularly the instructor, but somehow we struggled through. Aside from that, the Ox-Box was a nice easy aeroplane, once you had mastered its tendency to swing on take-off, and at about the same stage on landing, a distinct inclination to ground loop. Perhaps it was only because I was weighed down with all this gear and couldn't see properly that I noticed. If you can see and feel what is happening, you react instinctively and apply control so that a swing is countered before it develops, and no difficulty arises. It's hardly surprising that the instructors were bad tempered. However, I think that was, perhaps is, a characteristic of service flying instructors. This was something that had overtaken Training Command without their really knowing or being aware of it and had become accepted. But this tendency to abuse the pupils, to talk of them as 'pupes', to categorise them as slightly subhuman and treat them as if they had no feelings or were insensitive to criticism was widespread. I wonder if they still do it? I suspect they do. People I have met, involved in flying training or examining, particularly working for a regulating authority in civil aviation often revert to this type of behaviour when examining candidates and, if you trace it back, you will generally find that they had started as flying instructors in the service at some time.

And then I was posted to an OTU for training as a bomber pilot to start in earnest. Up till then I had always been part of a course, one of a group, such as a member of number nine course. And I was always among a different group of individuals, in a giant pack reshuffled at each stage. Although we arrived at OTU as members of a group and belonging to a course, this time it was different as we were to be sorted out as crews.

A little of the grand design became apparent. From training schools across the country and the Empire came groups of specialist trades. Pilots, navigators, bomb aimers, wireless operators and air gunners came together to be rearranged as crews. This was done with staggering simplicity. After a few days of lectures and visits to different parts of the aerodrome, of parades and CO's briefings, we were brought together inside a great hangar.

'Get yourselves sorted out', we were told. 'Come back to the desk with your names. This is what you need'. We knew what we needed, People started immediately to rush about, greeting each other, shaking hands and talking excitedly. I stood there looking about me. Presently, I found myself looking directly at a stocky, gruff-looking young man. He sported a navigator's badge and a bristly moustache. His uniform had been made for a standard-sized individual and roughly adapted to his unconventional shape. His shirt collar button had given up under the strain and was held around his neck by a tortured tie knot. He looked the despair of every drill sergeant and PT corporal that ever was. I recognised him as just the man I wanted and moved towards him. He came to meet me.

Unknowingly, I had drawn an ace. He was a Yorkshireman, and what's known in Yorkshire as a 'bit of a card'. He came from Leeds and his name was Geoff. 'What have you got?' he asked. 'Nothing', I said 'apart from a navigator'. 'Stay there', he said, 'you'll soon have a crew'. In short order, he assembled my crew. There was a dark and quiet Welshman for bomb aimer, another Yorkshireman, serious and good looking, for wireless operator, an Irishman from Belfast, fresh faced and good humoured for the mid-upper and the harum scarum Jock, with a wide and mischievous grin and a broad Scot's accent from Glasgow for rear gunner.

Number Fourteen OTU was located at Cottesmore, in County Rutland, England's smallest county, in which only recently a British government fell prey to the mania of name changing which had swept Africa, altered the boundaries and disappeared County Rutland. Number Fourteen OTU was equipped with Wellingtons. These were the brainchild of inventor and designer Barnes Wallis, and they had seen much service and better days. The unique feature of the Wellington was its geodetic metal construction. This was covered with doped fabric, which stretched and sagged with age. Visualise the skin of an elephant and you won't be far out. These planes were very early Wellingtons, Mark 1C, never noted for their performance and in the ageing process had deteriorated further. It was said by some that they only flew by virtue of flapping their wings. In the manner of the times, they were affectionately known as 'Wimpeys'.

Number Fourteen OTU must have done a pretty fair job. Even today, nearly forty years on, I could draw the schematic outline of the fuel system, although, never very good at figures, I might have to leave out the fuel quantities.

Heretofore, anything to do with flying had been very individual, with only an instructor to worry about. Now it was different. A whole gaggle of chaps had to be got ready, dressed up in flying suits and large, clumsy boots and laden with parachutes. They all had to be strapped in and plugged in to the intercom. Only then could we make a start. Naturally, the first part of the course, following the system's instruction, was learning to fly the aeroplane. Here the pilot was on display to his crew and, for everyone's sake, it was vital that things proceeded reasonably smoothly at this stage.

The flying instructors were an entirely new and different breed. They were men who had completed a tour of operations and had been stood down. The more recent of them came from Lancaster and Halifax squadrons, and others had operated in Wellingtons and Hampdens. Those who did the early part of the flying training on circuits and bumps had been given training as instructors for long enough to absorb the techniques of their trade, yet for a short enough time to avoid the attitudes that afflicted the instructors of Training Command.

We progressed smoothly through the course, from circuits to gunnery and bomb aiming and navigation, and left with a good average assessment. I was pleased with my crew and, I think, they with me. We worked well together. The instructors did their best to equip us for what was to come, although, as I was to say later, nothing in our experience or training had prepared us for the reality.

One further stage remained, the Heavy Conversion Unit. In autumn 1943 we arrived at Wigsley in Nottinghamshire for our final training before being posted out to an operational

The author in flying gear. The fleece-lined 'Sidcot Suit' could be worn over the pilot's uniform.

squadron. Over this long run-up, many things had changed or were changing.

Back in the dark days of early disasters, with the British armies routed and the Atlantic supply lines under increasing attack, with reverses and disasters sustained from the Middle East to Singapore, a bold plan to create a massive heavy bomber force to attack the German homeland and lay it waste had been conceived. But on the showing so far, this plan had met with scant success. Lack of suitable bombers, but more particularly, the huge lack of navigational systems to enable the bomber crews to locate and attack their targets had doomed the offensive to heavy losses and mediocre results.

The earlier enemy attacks on Britain, using only medium bombers and with no great weight of bombs, had the crucial advantage of navigational radio beams for crews to follow and intersect on their targets. The damage they had achieved gave cause for alarm. The RAF fighter command, making full use of their radio location equipment, clawed them from the skies over England and Hitler had turned away to launch his armies eastward in the most fateful battle of the war.

This gave the British the respite they needed. The bomber crews and the new heavy bombers were coming together on bases from Yorkshire to Lincolnshire, the worst defects and deficiencies in equipment were at last being made good, and the air marshals sensed their opportunity.

In what was, perhaps, the single most courageous decision and the boldest stroke of the war, Bomber Harris collected together his entire force, a thousand strong, and launched them against a single target, risking not only the main force but its very creators, in a single throw. Into the battle went training crews from the OTU's and conversion units, accompanied by their seasoned instructors. The consequences for Bomber Command, had it failed, would have been too awful to contemplate. But it succeeded beyond all expectation and now the die was cast. We had not advanced far enough in our training to take part, but our time was not far off.

At Wigsley we were joined by our flight engineer, fresh from his training at St Athan. He fitted in at once. Like farmers howling for binders at harvest time, the squadrons were howling for replacement bombers and crews to fly them. Wigsley had been stripped of serviceable Lancasters and was making do with a mixture of Lancasters and Halifaxes to train the crews. This worked surprisingly well. The instructors made good the deficiencies in our knowledge of the Halifax and its systems, we flew it at the speeds and conditions pertaining to the Lancaster and frankly, as we weren't that familiar with either, it served to cover another section of the syllabus. Towards the end we were judged sufficiently ready to omit most of the cross-country flights and we stood ready for posting.

One unfortunate setback spoils my memory of that time. By chance, upon the eve of our departure, the sergeants' mess arranged a party. Sergeants' mess parties are not things to attend lightly. To this day, accepting such an invitation should be done only after careful deliberation. They tend to run on and develop into wild affairs. This one was no exception. At some late hour, when the mess should have been closed, my navigator, Geoff Ward, was standing in the doorway surveying the room, a beatific smile on his face, when the Station Commander appeared, accompanied by an agitated duty officer. Like Tam o'Shanter before the auld kirk of Alloway, he stood amazed, though nothing memorable came to his lips. What circumstance had brought him to the mess we never knew. He buttonholed Geoff, demanding to know what was going on. Geoff's bonhomie expanded to incorporate the newcomers and welcome them to the festivities. 'That's my skipper over there', he said proudly, 'and that's my rear gunner dancing with him, I think that's a Highland Fling they're doing'. That wasn't quite

Air Vice Marshal Sir Ralph Cochrane.

accurate, it was an Eightsome Reel we had arranged, but I didn't hold it against him, it was probably not easy to tell. The outcome was that I had to appear in the CO's office the next morning. It was clear that he was still having difficulty in joining in the party spirit.

We were destined for Five Group, Bomber Command. This group was led by a man who was, perhaps, the most able and far-sighted of the bomber commanders.[1] He had decreed that his bomber pilots should be commissioned as part of his campaign for leadership and morale, either before, or shortly after, reaching his squadrons. Clearly, in the eyes of the Wigsley station commander I was not, at that time, a fit person to hold a commission and, as it turned out, he later marked my documents to recommend that my commission be deferred for six months. I dismissed the matter from my mind as we had serious work afoot and we dispersed on leave to reassemble in our squadron.

1 AVM Ralph Cochrane, who was to become influential in terms of Bomber Command tactics, took command of Five Group in October 1943.

A quiet tour

Number 61 Squadron, Bomber Command, was based at Syerston near Nottingham. I knew nothing about it, thinking it was just another main force squadron drawn at random with yet another sprog crew posted in. I did wonder a little about its history, but not in any serious way. In the squadron crest was a creature I took to be the Lincoln Imp, so it must have had some connection with the city of Lincoln. I believe that it was formed as a fighter squadron during the First World War as one of two such squadrons to defend London against threatened airship attacks, but whether it saw action then, I don't know. Nor did I know what, if anything, it had done in the intervening period.

It had been in business as a bomber squadron for some time, equipped originally with Hampdens. No very great success attended the Hampden. Worse was to follow. The squadron was re-equipped with Manchesters. Fortunately, these were so bad that they had to be redesigned. Fitted with four engines instead of two, and modified in other ways, the Manchester re-emerged as the Lancaster and was an instant success. It was superbly designed for its task and now takes its place, second only in public esteem, to the Spitfire. Joe Public may not know much about these things, but its surprising how often he gets it right.

It had the range required to strike deep into Germany while carrying a heavy bomb load, with the performance necessary to get it off the ground and up to 20,000 feet. It was easy to handle and fairly robust; necessary qualities when you consider the youth and inexperience of the vast majority of the pilots involved. If it had a serious defect it was that it was lightly armed and completely out-gunned by every enemy fighter. The RAF had somehow got stuck with its .303 calibre machine guns. Excellent though these had been in the early days of the war, they were now useless against heavier calibre guns and cannon shells. It may be that, in the long run this didn't matter and wouldn't have altered the outcome. But at the time, to the crews involved, it did matter. Fighter attacks were the most feared, although this was only one of the hazards facing the bomber crews. We counted ourselves lucky and straight away decided that No 61 was the best there was, if only because it was ours.

Our new squadron commander cast a jaundiced eye upon his latest acquisition, sprog crews, he gave us to understand, were a problem, especially those who'd had their training curtailed. Up to that point I had considered this something of a compliment, a point in our favour and not a defect. I ventured, as delicately as I could that this wasn't our doing; the squadrons needed crews urgently. That wasn't quite the whole message apparently. More better-trained crews, yes; not just more crews. Before we could start on operations, we would need more training, more cross-countries. He would see to it. He would also find us an easy trip to start with. Meantime we would have to wait until both these conditions could be fulfilled. The Group had been thinking about the problem of inexperience. Sprog crews tended to disappear and didn't last long enough to become experienced. Someone had hit on a good wheeze. Why not send the pilot and, perhaps, the navigator, as supernumeraries with an experienced crew? We could do that while waiting for the other training. I wondered silently what happened to the headless crews.

My navigator stole a march on me. He managed to get his supernumerary trip done first. 'What was it like?' we cried. 'Nothing to it', said Geoff, then went into great detail to show that there was a good deal to it. We spoke in the slang of the day. 'Give us the gen' and 'a piece of cake'.

I went off the next night with an experienced crew to Düsseldorf. They had done fifteen 'ops'. My logbook shows the date was 3 November 1943. It lists the crew and bomb load and a flight time of four hours forty minutes. Nothing in my training or previous experience had prepared me for the reality of this flight. We flew up the Ruhr valley in fine weather and a small amount of patchy cloud, turned on to the target heading and started the run in.

I was surprised by the amount of light from the city below, the burning incendiaries, target indicators and groping searchlights. The light rose in a vast glow illuminating the sky around us. I was dismayed by the apparent intensity of anti-aircraft fire. Gradually, it dawned on me that each shell burst formed its own puff of dark smoke and hung there suspended. The anti-aircraft gunners were busy trying to fill in the gaps between them. So this was flak. We flew through it, weaving and rocking about. It looked harmless enough. This must be a box barrage, I thought. Occasionally, one was close enough to be heard and that, I gathered, was far too close for comfort.

We were still weaving about when the bomb aimer started his run. He sounded very unhappy on the intercom. He appealed to the skipper: 'Left, left, for Christ's sake skipper, hold it steady, steady'. Then he chucked it. 'It's no good, skipper', he said, 'we'll have to go round again'. He called for bomb doors to be closed. We broke away to port, turning through 180 degrees. We were now flying into the bomber stream with flak coming up and bombs raining down. After what seemed an age, we turned back in again. This time the skipper made no attempt to weave, concentrating solidly on flying straight and level. The bomb aimer's 'left, left, steady', came through calm and unruffled. With, 'Bombs gone', and 'bomb doors closed', we turned away, the crew chatting to each other, pointing out this and that. We flew quietly back to a slightly bumpy landing at base.

We waited for the easy target the CO had promised. At Bomber Command they had other ideas. When they signalled 'maximum effort', we turned out with the others. At the briefing, all the details of the target were revealed, including the route, the turning points, the fuel and bomb loads. Each specialist took his turn fitting his part of the jigsaw to the picture. A vast and complex organisation had been at work to equip us right down to the last detail. All this was familiar from OTU days, but there was a indefinable difference of heightened awareness and tension. The scene itself was dramatic, with a lighted stage where the plot was revealed. But the audience were the actors about to play out their individual parts in a script that was as yet incomplete.

From the lights, warmth and company of the briefing, we kitted up and trooped out to the waiting transport to be delivered by the drivers to the dispersal. The aeroplane loomed large against the fading night sky and here the ground crew emerged from somewhere to brief us on the serviceability state and readiness. In so doing they handed over the aeroplane to us. Judging the timing, the skipper signalled an end to the chatter, the outside checks began, we clambered up the ladder to our stations, struggling across the main spar, the parachute pack heavy and awkward, causing the wearer to waddle like a duck. Strapped in and plugged in to oxygen and intercom, each man completed his individual checks and now the skipper called them up individually: 'captain to navigator', 'captain to bomb aimer'. For some it was first names, and most used the term 'skipper', but at this stage, I thought it best to keep formal, to bring them back from a descent into individuality and their personal fears to being a crew again, with the comfort that someone who bore the responsibility was in charge. If this helps the individual, in a curious way, it does more for the captain himself, bringing calm and resolution. Courage or bravery, or whatever it is that is needed to face danger, is more readily summoned in the company of others in a well-ordered, familiar routine. Something more is called for than a man alone, with only his own resources to draw upon.

A great many people, mistakenly, think we did brave things. I don't think we did. We did what we had volunteered and trained to do. Here and there, men did do brave things and Bomber Command was full of them. We basked at times in their reflected glory.

Neither let it be said that were we afraid. It is fashionable today, for people to deny brave acts. When asked, they say, 'I was scared stiff', 'I was petrified old boy'. To my mind this is fashionable nonsense. I don't say that all this passed through my mind as I sat that night in the left seat of a Lancaster, but at the beginning it did. I looked out at the airfield, aware that my mouth was dry, judging the time to start up. What looked like wisps of fog were forming on the airfield. I couldn't see the Trent Valley hidden at the end of the long runway, but I wondered what was happening there. Presently the recall signal went up from the control tower. The trip was scrubbed. Relieved, yet disappointed, we disembarked.

The CO was as good as his word. In short order, on the 5, 6 and 7 November, we dropped practice bombs by day on the range at Wainfleet and occupied the nights with cross-countries. These were code-named bullseyes and involved a little bit more than cross-country flying. Dummy attacks were made on various targets and the night-fighter force joined in with camera guns. The results from the bomb bay cameras were then scrutinised. We were pronounced ready. The easy trip came up. On 10 November we flew an air test and that night set out for Modane in the French Alps in M for Mike. The objective was to block the tunnel.

It was a fine night and we had no opposition. We had a splendid view of the mountains towering above us as we flew down the valley towards the mouth of the tunnel. With bombs away, we climbed out under maximum climb power, turning to avoid the peaks ahead and set course back to base. It took eight hours and twenty minutes' flying time. It was quite unremarkable and the fixed camera gave an aiming point photograph. The AOC was encouraging aiming point photographs and we each received a picture of a Lancaster with the crew names and date typed below, bearing AVM Cochrane's signature. I sent it to my mother, who kept it, so it survives to this day.

To have been on an easy trip, as easy as Modane, was no great shakes and I preferred to keep quiet about it. However, any such feelings were soon to be put right. I reflected that it

The author (2nd from right) with the crew of his Lancaster.

had taken me all but two years and two months to reach this point. I had accumulated a grand total of four hundred and twenty-six hours and five minutes prior to the first operation.

We paid another visit to Wainfleet and then ferried C for Charlie to our new base at Skellingthorpe, which we were to share with Number 50 squadron. I think we were all sad to trade Syerston and Nottingham for Skellingthorpe and Lincoln, and the move took up most of the rest of the month with further night-flying training and trying out a new rapid landing scheme.

Clearly, Five Group were busting a gut to raise the efficiency of their squadrons, to improve their bombing accuracy and navigation and get them back on the ground safely and expeditiously. On 19 November, one of our squadron aircraft returning from an operation ditched in the North Sea and we joined the search, flying below a ragged cloud base in a vain attempt to locate them.

In early December we made our first attack on Berlin in G for George. We didn't know it then, but we had been launched on the first of a series of attacks against the German capital that was to take up most of the winter of 1943–1944. This soon became evident to all, including the Germans, and the battle lines were drawn. This battle was clearly of the utmost importance to both sides. It seemed to me, as a newcomer to it all, that the odds were with the bombers. The Pathfinder force was becoming well established and equipped with navigation aids to enable them to find and mark their targets. Their techniques were forged in action and they were brilliantly led by Air Vice Marshal Donald Bennett, a most remarkable and experienced aviator. Although they had formed out of necessity and not as an elite, they were drawn from the ranks of battle-hardened and experienced crews in their mid-tour. The main force squadrons were now equipped with their new heavy bombers, Lancasters, Halifaxes and Stirlings.

Mosquitoes were being introduced in numbers for target marking and photo reconnaissance, and even as fighter escorts. We looked on this latter development sourly. To have to differentiate between the Mosquito silhouette and its opposite number in the night-fighter force was more than we were prepared to do.

At first, every man and his dog joined in. Although concerned primarily with our own affairs, we felt sorry for the Stirlings and Halifaxes struggling below with their shorter range and lower ceiling. Gradually, though no one told us, they were withdrawn from the battle, leaving the Lancasters with their longer range and heavier punch to carry the assault.

To the German defences, it was soon obvious what was afoot and at the briefings we were told that four thousand heavy guns, along with ten thousand light and medium guns, ringed the Big City. We had, perforce, to adopt the same route, time after time, until it became known as the tramlines. It must have been just as well known to the night-fighter force deployed to inflict the maximum damage on us. Using the techniques of spoof and diversionary raids to confuse the defences became increasingly unlikely to succeed as attack followed attack. The decisive factor was the weather. It should have been neutral, but to the bomber crews and particularly the Pathfinders, it didn't appear so. We needed one or two occasions with the target clear to start the fire storms and wreak a massive destruction.

Time after time, the weather obscured the city and forced the Pathfinders to use sky markers. These parachute flares, unless dropped with extreme accuracy and making due allowance for the wind drift, were a poor substitute for target indicators on the ground. The Germans were not above setting spoof fires around the city and lighting their own markers. The Pathfinders, taking the early brunt of the defences, didn't always survive to mark the target as planned, and the bomber crews, seeing nothing but the glow of fires through the overcast, were not inclined to dally and await further markers but bombed whatever they saw. The attacks also tended to trail back from the markers as crews, anxious not to stay too long so balefully exposed and under fire, bombed short and turned away for the comparative safety of the dark night skies.

Memory is a poor guide and very fallible. In all this, my flying logbook gives hard detail of dates and places, bomb loads and flight times. Some things are forgotten or half-remembered, or are distorted and out of sequence. Other things are recalled with great clarity, although hindsight must also play a part. It was obvious, however, from the number of trips we did to the Big City that our masters were not content. If we had destroyed the city they would not have wished to go on turning over the rubble. In this sequence, we had a little light relief with a trip to Frankfurt and one to Stettin. This latter was the longest we did: nine hours and twenty-five minutes. Under the logbook column, 'DUTY' including 'Results and Remarks', I have noted, 'Port wheel failed to lock down on return'. This is a rather unsatisfactory remark as it was, presumably, only an indication fault, but it does help to show that we were having what was known as a quiet tour. By that I mean we were not hit or injured or shot to pieces. Although subject to the same dangers as the others, we had come through, so far, unscathed.

The Frankfurt trip, however, turned nasty. It was a fine night and very dark. Outbound towards the target the calm was broken by a sudden alert from the rear gunner. Out of the pitch black below came the silhouette of a night fighter filling his sights and breaking away to port and above us. Undetected, he had made his approach and, by some quirk of fate, some failure on his part, or of his equipment, not a shot had been fired. The realisation of what might have been cast a chill of fear upon us that went through the aeroplane. I urged them to keep a look-out and made one or two small turns to scan below in a gesture of defiance, but to little purpose.

Approaching Frankfurt, the defences were coming alive and the first flak bursts made their appearance. Immediately alongside us a scarecrew exploded. It looked like an aircraft taking a direct hit, shattering in fragments, then hanging in the sky instead of plummeting earthwards. I reassured them easily, myself included. 'It's all right, only a scarecrew'.

We flew on towards the target. The searchlights were groping for a victim to show him up for the prowling fighters or for the anti-aircraft gunners. A searchlight beam caught us momentarily and overshot, then came back to lock us in its blinding light. His friends came sweeping across to join him and form the cone. I pushed down in my seat, snapped the panel lights to maximum and started to corkscrew for dear life. For a moment we were caught but in our initial steep diving turn we slipped out of the noose and they never really held us again. Reduced to the immediate world of the blind flying panel in front of me, I laid in maximum bank angle and rate of descent, changing from dive to climb, holding in the bank, scanning the dials, trading height and speed, rolling from maximum bank one way to maximum the other, striving for accuracy with maximum effect, while keeping the wings on. When it seemed that he had truly lost us, we settled back to level flight and prepared for the attack.

Taffy seemed well pleased with the run, so the gyros must have settled down also and we turned away on to the first heading for home. Thirty-five years later, I read a book about Bomber Command that my wife had brought from the library. It was a most authentic account of that time and I read with interest of places and things I had known and shared. Then I had a shock. Despite the author's researches of German war material and records, he had come up empty-handed on the subject of scarecrews. No such wonderful pyrotechnic had ever existed.

On 19 February we went to Leipzig. We were routed as though taking the tramlines to Berlin. To keep the bomber stream together and assist the navigation, a wind-finding system was under trial. Although we were not especially equipped for it, we had been designated as wind finders. On the long haul out over the North Sea and in the climb to altitude, we knew ourselves to be on track as we buffeted around in the comforting slip stream of unseen aeroplanes, and Geoff was busy fixing on the GEE navigation system.

He passed the figures up to me and he seemed troubled. 'It's unbelievable', he said, 'a very strong westerly. If we send this back they won't believe it'. We discussed it for a while, debating whether to cut it back or not. In the end I decided to send it back unmodified. After all, the idea was to combine all the winds found, fit them to the synoptic situation and transmit a composite wind back to the bomber force. Sure enough, it came back modified, the wind speed considerably reduced. We droned on through the night towards the enemy coast. Geoff gave me two ETAs for the turning point. The first was his own, based on the wind he had found, and the second was based on the composite. The operational plan was very simple. We appeared to be heading for Berlin. When we came abeam of Leipzig we were to turn off for our real target. It was clear that we would overshoot the turning point.

You can't actually do much to alter an aircraft's cruising speed. It's a narrow range, limited at the top by the power available and, at the bottom, by the need to keep sufficient airflow over the wings to stay above the stall. In this narrow band there is an optimum where the lift/drag ratio is at its most favourable. To circle within the bomber stream was not a technique I favoured, but nearer the time, I was prepared to put in a dog leg.

Barely had we crossed the enemy coast when the port inner engine failed and had to be shut down. I decided to carry on. By hand-flying as carefully and accurately as I could, we kept the height loss within bounds and the slight reduction in airspeed was to our benefit. I decided that we would promote ourselves to the first wave, turn on Geoff's ETA and risk getting there early and, if need be, stooge about when we reached Leipzig, or put in a dog leg just before. It had the hallmarks of a shambles.

We did our little dog leg and made it smack on time. I was two hundred feet short of our regular height of twenty thousand feet when we bombed and I was particularly proud of that. The trip, and its return were otherwise uneventful. There was one difference at debriefing. A senior high-ranking officer was present and was taking an interest. He questioned us for a little while, perhaps because nothing of greater interest offered that night. Geoff affected great indignation over the modification to his wind finding, but no one took him up on it.

In all, we did nine trips to the Big City, starting in early December, the last one in mid-February 1944. I feel a little uneasy, as I have told people that we did ten, but that was because one of them never took place and, as it didn't, it gets no mention as a logbook entry. Our regular aeroplane was G for George, although occasionally, we operated in M for mother. The aeroplanes were not allocated exclusively to one crew. When we stood down or went on leave others flew them. G for George had landed away and it was decided that we would position there and operate as part of another squadron, returning to our own base afterwards. I'm not even sure where this was, but Waddington comes to mind. I recall that it was an Australian squadron. We had a fair sprinkling of Dominion (Commonwealth) aircrew on Number 61, but there were very few Aussies and stories were circulating at the time that all these Dominion squadrons were a bit ropy. This was the kind of rumour that was spread and believed, even if it was entirely without foundation. It is true to say that we were a bit prejudiced and took our place at briefings feeling slightly superior. This characteristic of the British has failed to endear us to our colonial cousins over the years. We trooped out to our machine and made ready.

I watched the first aeroplane take-off, thundering by fairly close to our dispersal, then lumbering skyward, his navigation lights gradually fading in the distance. One or two more followed. We had been set a precise time for start up and departure. I called the ground crew chief to start up and a mechanic climbed into the starboard wheel well to prime the KI gas pump.[1] I watched casually, as the next aeroplane started his take-off run and came towards us. All at once I could see that he was swinging off the runway and careering towards us. We were right in his path. I shouted a futile warning. On the flight deck, we ducked down behind the coaming in an even more futile gesture. He must have continued turning as he thundered past, taking part of our starboard wing with him. We scrambled out, forgetting the mechanic in the wheel well, and ran for cover, or just fell flat on the grass. I don't know how long I lay there in the open, but presently, I recovered from my fright, got to my feet and set off towards the wreckage. It had come to rest between a hangar and some sort of shelter and other paraphernalia. All was quiet. I couldn't leave them there, trapped inside, even if they *were* Aussies. I scrambled inside and made my way forward. The aeroplane was deserted. I turned and made my way back out. On the way, I met my navigator coming forward on the same ploy. 'They've gone', I said. 'Not a bad idea', he said, 'this bloody lot could go up any minute'.

We collected everyone together and made our way back to the briefing room. There was no one about. We rustled up some transport and made our way back to base. Last we heard, they had located all the crew, and the rear gunner was found

1 System of starting engines by injecting fuel, in the form of a mist, into the intake pipe.

wandering across the airfield, distressed because he had got his intercom plug wet.

In our usual way, we made nothing of it. There was, of course, no debriefing and no one interested. We were not a very satisfactory crew at debriefings anyway, preferring to get it over and get to the eggs and bacon, and off to bed. I don't know who the people were, referred to by the BBC, who left targets blazing and so you could see them lighting up the sky a hundred miles behind them. We concentrated on accurate navigation and keeping up a sharp look out till it was time to descend over the North Sea and then, free of the need for oxygen, someone would take Jock a coffee and light a fag for him and then come to full alert again for the last bit, on a safe arrival at base.

There was another occasion that fortunately also came to nothing. We were briefed for Königsberg. Perhaps this was at Uncle Joe's request. The ribbon joining East Anglia to the target looked longer than usual. Before the briefing ended, my navigator had cross-checked the fuel figures against the distance and time that would elapse. He began to nudge me persistently, insisting that I get to my feet and say something. His calculations showed that we could make it all right, but would run out of fuel somewhere over the North Sea on the return. Failing a sensible answer, he wanted charts and details of suitable landing grounds in Sweden. It got embarrassing all round.

Somewhere, someone found an out, common sense prevailed and the trip was scrubbed. We concluded that it must have been a political or propaganda stunt of some kind, that the air marshals were under pressure they couldn't resist and had, perforce, to resort to finding some last-minute technicality to call it off.

This episode left a nasty taste in the mouth. We were aware that those in authority doubted us at times, suspecting the onset of what they called 'LMF', or 'lack of moral fibre', either as individuals or as whole squadrons. It was clear, when attacks failed, that these figures might question the reasons for it, believing it due to the lack of a 'press on' spirit. As evidence, one could cite the trail back from the markers, the incidence of early returns with technical defects and, perhaps most significant and a nasty feature of that time, the jettisoning of the cookie into the North Sea on the way out. We reported this each time we saw it occur; the strange flash at a time when flashes were not expected. There were either a lot more technical failures than one might expect, or the boys were cheating. When the cameras were re-rigged to operate whenever the bomb doors opened, this phenomena ceased. But Königsberg caused a reverse doubt, just a suspicion. Was it possible it might have gone ahead? My navigator's figures were, as usual, beyond doubt. Later in the war, Königsberg was bombed. They must have found space for more fuel than we were offered.

In January, we left Skellingthorpe for Coningsby, which was a distinct improvement in locality though it was still in Lincolnshire. Boston became our nearest town, and it was much friendlier and not so swamped with aircrew as Lincoln.

The first two weeks of February was taken up with bombing practice, searchlight and fighter affiliation, beam approaches and corkscrews. The corkscrew was an essential evasive manoeuvre intended to make life difficult for an attacker by refusing him the opportunity of a no-deflection shot. The name explains itself. I always felt sorry that no one thought up a better name for it. In the skies over Texas, I had, assiduously practised manoeuvres with romantic names like Immelmann. The Immelmann was a manoeuvre credited to the First World War German fighter ace of the same name. Perhaps the Second World War aviators were less romantic or less inventive than their predecessors.

The senior officer at the Leipzig debriefing must have taken more interest than I realised, for shortly thereafter, I received promotion to commissioned rank along with the immediate award of a Distinguished Flying Medal. He must also have outranked my friend at Wigsley as I had still two months' deferment to run. We celebrated with a dinner and drinks at the Leagate public house nearby and our ground crew came too. The evening was financed with the gratuity from the medal that was paid with the promotion. At the same time came an invitation to join the Pathfinders. Unfortunately, this included only myself and my navigator and mysteriously didn't extend to the rest of the crew. Apart from the fact that a tour with the Pathfinders extended to forty-five operations, fifteen more than the main force tour, we easily decided that we didn't want to split up. Along with the gratuity money, that issue was disposed of at the Leagate public house.

We settled down to a further series of operations over Germany with Schweinfurt and Stuttgart twice, a repeat visit to Frankfurt, then Essen and Nuremberg. The Nuremberg flight was to see a turning point in our affairs. On a clear night, just south of the Ruhr valley, we were set upon by two night fighters. They took up position, one on each side. To all intents, we were a dead duck. Our corkscrew manoeuvre only served to expose us to the second attacker as we turned towards the first. By some unknown means, however, their co-ordination broke down and they failed to take advantage. We continued weaving, drawing them deeper into Germany and, hopefully, further from their base. When they left us as suddenly as they came, we had lost track of our navigation. We continued as though nothing had happened and I decided to go to our original ETA plus ten minutes. We had used up a deal of extra fuel. It seemed likely that we would be sufficiently close to see the attack begin and join in. The ETA came and went. There was no sign of any warlike activity. As we approached the ten minute deadline I had set, a searchlight came on and started groping for us. An anti-aircraft battery opened up on us. As nothing else offered, I decided they could have the benefit of our full attention. We turned towards them and started our bombing run. Shortly after 'bombs gone', the searchlight went off and the gunfire ceased. We turned for home. There was an excited call from Jock in his rear turret. He could see the attack begin behind us. We had turned too soon.

The winds must have changed and we were running late. We must have been fairly close to track. It was too late now:

we would be back early and have to make what excuses we could at debriefing. At the debriefing, they seemed concerned with other things and relieved to see anyone safely back. Reports of heavy losses were coming in. We had survived what was subsequently known to be the worst night of the war for Bomber Command.

Whether the last event brought about the change, or whether the softening up for the coming invasion of Europe was started a little early, I never knew. With the coming of April we turned our attention to the easier targets in France and obtained a string of aiming point photographs. We also returned to Skellingthorpe. In between, the practice bombing flights continued, now transferred to a place called Epistone. On 1 April I noted, 'Eight bombs. Error 51 yards from 20,000 feet'. This must have been a very good result to get this special mention. Our usual mixture of incendiary bombs, plus one 1,000 pound cookie, was now changed to all high explosives. Ten 1,000 pound bombs for Toulouse, fourteen for the marshalling yards at Tours, fifteen for Aachen. We were also bombing from lower levels for greater accuracy, which reflected the lack of opposition. An occasional trip to Germany kept us from getting too relaxed and once or twice things turned nasty at the 'easy' targets.

About this time, Five Group was becoming known as the Independent Air Force. Perhaps dissatisfied with the Pathfinders, or inclined to believe that they could achieve better results with their own system of marking, they were given the OK to demonstrate what they could achieve.

On 3 May a small force of Lancasters set out to attack a tank training school at Mailly-le-Camp in France. The target was marked by red spot fires laid by Group Captain Cheshire at very low level. Radio communication was to be used to direct the bombers and yellow sky markers dropped for them to circle while waiting for the master of ceremonies to call them in. Six thousand feet was the bombing height, with 12,250 pounds of high explosive as the bomb load.

One or two little things went awry. From somewhere or other,

Flight Lieutenant Charles Jeffrey Gray.
Distinguished Flying Medal, *Légion d'honneur.*

the enemy night fighters got interested, attracted perhaps by the brilliant sky markers. Certainly, it soon appeared as if there were nearly as many of them as the Avro Lancasters circling the markers. When the leader had his red spot fires laid, he called in the first wave of bombers. Hardly had he spoken than we were on our bombing run with bombs away. Jock gleefully reported that we'd hit them fair and square, we'd blown the markers out, blown them sky high.

As we bent the throttles for home, we could hear the master of ceremonies calling off the attack until more markers could be laid, among words of protest arising from the circling bombers. The night fighters said nothing but set about their business with renewed ferocity. The losses for such a small affair were severe and no doubt gave rise to serious soul-searching at Five Group headquarters.

We began to worry about having so many easy targets. The word was out that these wouldn't count as full operations, only counting as half, or even a third. This seemed very likely, and certainly a practical step to take. What had seemed an impossible number now began to look like a piece of cake. With the darling buds of May starting to blossom, we were getting very close to our thirty operations, so the matter was of some importance to us.

On 8 May, in an attack on what I remember as the submarine pens at Brest, we were hit by flak for the first time. My logbook corrects this faulty remembrance and quite clearly names 'Lanvéoc-Poulmic seaplane base, near Brest' as the target. The flak did some slight damage to the port mainplane and knocked out the starboard outer engine. We turned for home, ignoring the route laid down, which took us out to sea away from possible pursuit, and laid a course direct. It was as well that we did because, on the way, another engine gave trouble, losing its coolant and overheating and had to be shut down. We arrived home first on two engines and forgot to make a big deal of it. Instead, I complained that the aeroplane seemed sloppy and imprecise. I expect that I was worried about unseen damage. The night was bumpy and perhaps I was unused to flying any distance under two engines. For whatever reason, the CO decided to test fly the aeroplane himself when the repairs were carried out. Needless to say, he found it faultless and I thought I caught him looking at me suspiciously.

At Bourg-Léopold, a military camp in Belgium, we failed

to identify the target and, complying with our instructions, returned and landed with 11,500 pounds of high explosive on board, having jettisoned two 1,000 pounders in the North Sea. That one certainly shouldn't have counted, and it was number twenty-nine.

We now began a series of exercises involving air to sea firing, formation flying and low-level bombing at 500 and 1,000 feet. I felt they might have further plans for us. On 19 May we returned to the marshalling yards at Tours with another 13,000 pounds of what my logbook describes as a general-purpose high explosive.

We awaited the decision. Wing Commander Doubleday told me the good news. All the trips were to count. We were tour-expired. We broke up and went our various ways, a chapter ended. We expressed the hope we would come together for another tour, knowing it to be unlikely, but if we could, we would try. We'd had a quiet tour and were proud of it. If we had brought no great glory to No 61, we had been, very much, a main force crew, and we had not disgraced them. We had rubbed shoulders with men who had done heroic things and been acknowledged. My friend Tommy Farmiloe was embarrassed by a banner headline in his local newspaper, 'Birmingham Boy Bombs Berlin in Blazing Bomber'. I rather liked it, although the accompanying story was the usual garbled newspaper stuff. Tommy ran into engine trouble. He wound up with one shut down and another run away. They were unable to feather the propeller and the engine caught fire. He continued to the target, barely able to keep control, with two engines operative on one side and the massive drag from the runaway propeller on the other. With the bombs gone, they turned for home and steadily losing height set a course direct for East Anglia. The engine fire died down to a red glow and eventually went out.

He got his bomb aimer to rig a rope to the rudder pedals to assist him in maintaining control and, flying just above the stall speed, he initially planned to put distance between him and the target before ordering his crew to bale out. Quite how he himself would get out was a problem which he hadn't resolved.

Their course took them over a defended area and they came under fire. Unable to weave or manoeuvre and barely staying airborne, they progressed towards the coast, desperately husbanding every foot of altitude. Over the North Sea and now down to 2,000 feet, he changed the plan to ditching, but meantime, soldiered on. With the double engine failure had come problems of failed electrics and hydraulics. They were unable to get off a distress call and their IFF (Identification Friend or Foe) was inoperative. A convoy proceeding on its appointed way up the North Sea took exception to their passage and opened fire. They crossed the coast of East Anglia and the coastal defences confirmed it with another hostile reception. Tommy now revised his plan once more and cast about for a suitable landing place. With any luck the gear would extend on the emergency air bottle and, if he kept up his speed and power to maintain flying control, he just might get the thing down in one piece. Some unknown unit was night flying. The Drem[2] and runway lights were on. Unable to make any sort of radio contact, his colours of the day cartridges gone in the earlier vain attempts to identify themselves as friendly, Tommy lined up for a long approach, fearful that some alert control officer would douse the lights. His luck held. He got it down to a very respectable landing. The problem now was how to stop. He'd had to carry excess speed to keep control and the pneumatics were gone and, with them, the brakes. They trundled off the far end, ran up an embankment and ground to a halt, the nose overhanging a canal. They sat there for some time collecting their gear and their wits. One of them nearly fell into the canal. That would have capped it, thought Tommy, to come all that way and survive so many hazards, to drown in a canal in East Anglia.

I think he was even more embarrassed to receive a DSO. Tommy was one of that rare and delightful breed of Englishman, modest and self-deprecating, a master of under statement.

2 A system of shrouded lights that could be dimmed, making them invisible to enemy aircraft. Named after RAF Drem, where the system was developed.

Along with so many such things of value that has vanished in the post-war world of England, these qualities have become rarer still. Tommy went on quietly to complete the tour.

I hardly know 'Jock' Reid. The trip that won him the Victoria Cross, and his engineer the Conspicuous Gallantry Medal, was one of great courage and endurance. Looking at the damage to the aeroplane and piecing the story together in the mess, I was not surprised to hear that our sister squadron at Coningsby, Number 617 squadron of the Dam Busters fame, wanted him.

He came under fighter attack crossing the coast outbound and suffered severe damage. Although injured and with his crew either injured or dead and dying, he continued to the target and brought his stricken Lancaster home. With the cockpit open to the slipstream and no instrument panel to speak of, he flew and navigated by what stars could be seen. On the approach to land, the blood which had congealed and frozen from a head wound, began to run down his face and into his eyes. His flight engineer, acting as his eyes, talked him down the approach and together they made it back to base.

I heard later that he was posted missing on a raid on a flying bomb site, shot down by flak. Only two parachutes were seen to open. He was, however, a hard 'chiel to ding' and the last time I heard of him he was alive and well and living in his Bonny Scotland. And who can say what acts of courage and daring were performed, unrecognised, by those who failed to return; who 'got the chop', or went for a 'Burton', in the slang of our time. Somehow, the next morning, the people whose job it was to collect up their effects would appear and unobtrusively pack away their kit, leaving a row of empty beds along one side of a Nissen hut in mute testimony.

Roll on the boat

After this they did a very nice thing and proved themselves human and understanding after all. They posted me back to my old OTU where I had been a trainee. Even better was to come when one or two of them said they remembered me. They'd moved from County Rutland to Market Harborough, and next door to Market Harborough was Leicester. If Nottingham was my first love among English cities, Leicester came pretty close to it. Like Tigger, I found what it was that I really liked. It was instructing. They still had Wellingtons but not the same ones. The old Mark lCs had been replaced by Mark Xs. When I had been checked out again and I'd done a spell as a screen pilot, I was sent off to Upavon and a flying instructor's course. That pretty well sealed my fate.

Life on an OTU was very pleasant. One course succeeded another over the same routine. Quite early on I found that I had a marked diagnostic ability. If someone had a problem with his flying I could usually uncover it and, in so doing, put it right. At Market Harborough I soon acquired a reputation, and it followed that I got more than my fair share of problem children. This brought its own rewards. Being able to sort things out and then see the student change visibly and begin to progress is immensely satisfying. At this stage in the game failures were very rare, as the weeding out had been done beforehand, and so I was spared the agony and heart-searching that failure brings in train. We worked hard, though not unduly so, and had spare time and leave in plenty. Something of the bomber squadrons reflected on us. Occasionally we went out with a crew as a screen pilot if they were judged too raw to be allowed out by themselves and, almost certainly, we accompanied them if they were used as spoofs to simulate a bomber raid.

On one such occasion I had to accompany a crew on a diversionary raid. The route took us out over the North Sea. Before reaching the enemy coast, we were to return and proceed back to base. My particular crew looked a promising lot and we took off from Harborough and set course as planned. Radio silence had, of course, to be observed, although we had to maintain a listening watch in case of recall or diversion. Whether our wireless operator misinterpreted this and had his receiver switched off, or whether it was truly unserviceable, as he later claimed, I was never to know and I decided that it was better all round if I believed him. It so happened that the weather forecast was doubtful and, unknown to us, as we climbed away on track, the main bomber offensive was stood down and scrubbed for the night. Shortly thereafter, the diversionary raid laid on by the OTUs was also scrubbed and those aeroplanes already airborne were recalled. All, that is, except one tour-expired bomber pilot and his trainee crew in their Wellington bound for their scheduled turning point off the coast. We set off alone on our diversion. Also unknown to us, the Met's prediction of fog began to be realised and the recall signals went unheard.

The absence of slip streams should have alerted me, as the navigation was good and the GEE worked well, but no suspicion of anything untoward entered my mind till we arrived back at base. 'The Drem lights have a funny look', I thought, as we followed them round. From overhead they seemed bright enough, but at any distance they blurred rapidly. Fog! The airfield was fogging in, or had already done so. My chap was flying very well but he didn't have a chance. On the approach as we turned in, the lights dimmed and disappeared from view. He was apologetic. 'Not your fault, old lad', I told him, 'let's see if I can do better'. We went round again and I talked to them quietly. A diversion to East Anglia was probably the best bet and, in particular, I favoured Bircham Newton near King's Lynn. I favoured it because I'd very recently completed an SBA[1] course there on blind approaches. Perhaps the crew would be good enough to get things ready while I made another approach. It was no more successful than the first. We set off for East Anglia. There was a bad moment or two when the navigator thought that he had lost the flimsy, the legendary piece of rice paper which gave us our diversionary codes, without which we'd not find Bircham Newton. After a brief panic he found it again. 'Ah well', I thought, 'I might get my chance to 'hit the silk' after all'. I'd have preferred a more heroic set of circumstances. At Bircham Newton however, they were night flying using their blind approach, so we joined in and landed and groped our way to dispersal.

Next day, after a good night's sleep, we returned to base in clear weather. I entered up the wireless receiver as U/S in the Form 700. I'd like to think that it was my aptitude as an instructor but, whatever the reason, all my applications to return to operations, were turned down; blocked I suspect, by the chief flying instructor. I doubt if they ever got beyond his in tray. I must have shown perseverance in these applications, as I see from my logbook that I passed the Mosquito squadron decompression tests in the tank at Upper Heyford with 'no ill effects or symptoms'. And so it was that I missed the invasion of Europe. Even now, I feel a tinge of regret.

When the war in Europe ended, I was still pounding the circuit turning out bomber crews. Number 14 OTU was shortly to be disbanded and I found myself posted to Number 17 at Silverstone, where they lost no time in banishing me to the satellite field. From there I was to make one more trip to Germany.

At that time, the RAF were running sightseeing trips to look at the damage. Although the Wellington was hardly designed to offer anything of a lookout, I took one to the Ruhr Valley and Cologne. Once again, I was unprepared for the awful devastation, the torn, broken buildings, and certainly unprepared for the cathedral, standing solidly amid the

1 Standard Beam Approach (SBA) was a blind-landing radio navigation system.

flattened streets in awesome reproach.

I had to wangle my way into Transport Command. Much as I enjoyed being an instructor, I found it increasingly frustrating to go on producing bomber crews. Some bright Herbert gave me the clue. 'Tuesdays', he said, 'Transport Command headquarters at Bushey Park. They're interviewing every Tuesday. As long as you have the hours'. I had the flying hours. It may not have been a Tuesday: it might have been a Wednesday. No matter, acting on this information, I arranged a day off for the very next week and, at the time given, presented myself at Transport Command headquarters, wearing my best blues and armed with my flying logbook. Fate, in mischievous mood, took a hand. I joined a group of similarly attired junior officers in the outer hallway. An NCO bearing a clipboard appeared and called out names. To my astonishment, he called 'Flight Lieutenant Gray'. Two of us stepped forward in response. Clearly there had been a cock-up at records. A further check on service numbers resolved it. I assured the NCO that I had been instructed to appear, I had the hours and insisted that it be put to the selection board. They agreed to see me. I was in. Could I report at Riccall to start my course on Monday? Certainly I could. I cleared up any likely difficulty. It would probably take a few days for the posting notice to come through. I would need to start clearing the station straight away, without authority. The chairman brushed aside such trivial matters. 'Refer them to me', he said.

I went off to lunch with my namesake to buy him a beer. I remember he had a very pretty SS Jaguar motor car. I consoled him on his posting to Dakotas. Apparently, he hadn't got the hours for the heavy stuff. I also located Riccall in Yorkshire. I told him the truth of the matter years later.

Clearing the station proved the usual difficulty. You had to do the rounds of each section, obtaining signatures as you went. This could be quite pleasant, or sometimes sad and, if your affairs were not in order, it could cause problems. My affairs were not in order, as no official posting notice existed, nor was it likely to in the time available. I had to resort, in the end, to a little forgery, the time-honoured way of clearing a station. I was hampered, moreover, in that my bicycle had disappeared, a not-uncommon fate for personal possessions in those days. I had, perforce, to write it off, along with the more difficult signatures, and proceed to Yorkshire.

At Riccall another problem emerged. I remembered the headless crew problem in Bomber Command. This was the converse. While ex-bomber crews arrived complete, minus air gunners and bomb aimers, or people had been posted in, to make up complete crews, I had arrived on my own. I therefore set about finding a crew. On every station there were bodies left over for a variety of reasons and you merely had to locate them. Station sick quarters was a good place to start. I found two crew members there. It was enough to be going on with.

The training went well. The aeroplane we were to fly was a York. Somewhere towards the end of the war, when people began to look beyond the immediate aim, it was realised that Britain would start the piping days of peace with a lot of clapped out, and quite unsuitable aeroplanes, and something would have to be done to remedy this. We had, in fact, got ourselves in a bad fix and it never was completely remedied.

As a temporary fix, A V Roe had designed a box car fuselage, stuck Lancaster wings and engines on it and dubbed it the York. It worked well enough and was a grand workhorse and, at the time, I was quite thrilled by it. For our passing out exercise, we made a trip to Rabat in North Africa. This was my first venture into the post-war world outside Britain and I was immediately entranced by it. But the most persistent impression was that of shortages. The local lads were anxious to buy anything, particularly clothing, and could offer good money for whatever you stood up in. Realising the impracticability of that, they hung about the transit place making offers for shirts and underwear and anything that might be spared.

We set off back with our squadron leader invigilator. I hadn't realised it yet, but I had been blessed, yet again, with an ace navigator and this was soon to be revealed. Up there in Yorkshire, fog was blanketing our base and we were instructed as to diversions.

Cloud obscured the night sky and navigational aids were sparse to the point of non-existence. Neglecting nothing that came to hand, Mulholland, my navigator, took a series of shots on the moon seen through the hazy cloud above and eventually got a radio bearing. Running up his last moon shot, he was able to produce a reliable fix for the start of the let-down, confirming it on crossing an instrument landing beam, and we were able to proceed to a safe landing at Merryfield with every confidence that we knew where we were and what we were doing. Clearly, our invigilator was most impressed by this display of competency and initiative and we felt we had made a very good start.

We took off for Riccall the next day. The fog had cleared and, after so successful a trip, my crew and I also cheered up. We lifted skywards from Merryfield's runway in great good humour.

We were posted to a training squadron at Holmsley, hidden away in the New Forest in Hampshire. This was a pleasant spot, if a little damp in the winter of 1945. There we began to learn our business, which was to help bring home the great armies of troops left by the tides of war in India and the Far East. There was more training to come: a course on radio range flying, and BABS[2] and SBA, the two main methods of homing and blind approach at that time. We did two trooping flights, venturing as far as Calcutta on the first and Karachi on the second, before being cleared for full passenger services and posting to Number 511 squadron at Lyneham.

At first, once again, every man and his dog joined in. All manner of ex-bomber and coastal and transport squadrons were involved, regardless of the suitability or otherwise, of their equipment. Periodically, Number 511 had to interrupt its schedules of regular services to tackle the logjams that occurred at places such as Tripoli, Malta and Lydda. Aeroplanes went U/S or were damaged in 'hairy' arrivals, leaving groups of

---

2 The Beam Approach Beacon System (BABS): a radio homing device used to help pilots land in reduced visibility.

stranded passengers to be brought home.

Number 511 squadron had things well organised using existing RAF bases throughout the Mediterranean and the Middle East to India, Ceylon and Singapore. Our customers seemed to me to be a moaning lot. They'd been away from home for a long time. Some had endured the most frightful hardships at the hands of the Japanese or had fought in forgotten armies in the jungles of the Far East. Others had sweated it out on soft and cushy numbers in India, with boredom as their greatest enemy. In addition to the moaning, they had one other thing in common: the desire to get home. Their main subject of conversation was demob dates and groups and they endeared themselves to us with remarks like, 'get some in' and 'get your knees brown'.

I have to admit that the crews newly out from the UK were a sorry sight. The RAF, being the junior service and perhaps rather hurriedly put together, hadn't got around to considering service in warmer climates and providing suitable clothing. The army-style khaki shorts were long and wide in the leg and the bush jackets really set them off. After a hot, sticky departure, you dried out at altitude and got very cold. At the end of the sector, the stores garb had formed and when you stood up, it remained seated. We noticed that the old hands had encountered the same problem and dealt with it in their own way. The local tailors were willing to tackle anything and had cheerfully helped design and manufacture a whole range of tropical uniforms. Perhaps the most noticeable garment to emerge at this time was the Betty Grable. The wonder of this exclusively RAF garment was that more didn't emerge. The cut, style and colour of the cloth varied with each and every tailor. They looked an extraordinary mob but anyone could see that they had got their knees brown.

All along the route, at the various bases and stations, there were key personnel to handle and service the aircraft. They, too, were interested in demob groups and numbers; some particularly so, as their release dates had to be deferred to keep the aircraft operating. Eventually, this rising tide of discontent broke through in a quite unprecedented manner and we were caught up in it.

Leaving Cairo for the next stage through Shaibah to Karachi, some of the ground crew took me aside. It was all rather mysterious. 'Captain', they said, 'you'll probably get stuck at Shaibah and certainly at Mauripur. They're all coming out on strike at midnight tonight'. They tried to persuade me to stay put. No they weren't taking part in a strike, not in Cairo; it was the Far East. The whole thing was expected to grind to a halt in protest against deferment. Unbelieving, I elected to press on. At Shaibah we were met but there was some reluctance to refuel and see the flight on its way. There was doubt, however, about which midnight was set for the strike. Although it was now past the local midnight, it was not yet midnight GMT. I played upon this point and so it was that we were refuelled and proceeded on our way. At Mauripur, Karachi, things were very quiet and the airfield well-nigh deserted. The duty officer in the tower explained: the officers were still working but the airmen had downed tools and gone on strike. There was some doubt as to whether the NCOs had joined them or not. He had given us landing directions and a parking place but whether we would get any further service was doubtful.

We were quite prepared to arrange things ourselves but, eventually, a truck pulled up with an officer driver to take us to the transit camp. We jumped in and found ourselves some vacant charpoys to get some sleep and await events.

When I surfaced the next day, the camp was curiously quiet. People were wandering about rather aimlessly and no one seemed to know exactly what was happening. Rumour had it that a senior officer was arriving from Delhi that afternoon and would address the camp. An assembly was planned for four o'clock to hear him. I'm sorry I didn't attend but, clearly, officers weren't involved and might not have been welcome. There didn't appear to be any outcome. Many of the people attending drifted off during the address and those who stayed didn't think anything new had been added. The authorities seemed to be as perplexed by the situation as the rest of us.

The strike began to peter out the next day and I was able to put aside the tentative plans I had made for refuelling and loading.

Long afterwards, I heard that some of the signals staff in Delhi were singled out for court martial as instigators. It must have been very awkward. You can't have a strike in the services: you have to call it mutiny. This strange little episode received scant attention in the press and was soon forgotten.

The shortages that had been brought to my attention in Rabat were evident elsewhere, taking different forms and to greater or lesser degrees. Where such conditions exist, people who are enterprising by nature come forward to try and bring supply and demand into balance. There were such people in Transport Command. Once again, the choice of name was important. 'Unauthorised trading' was the term generally used, shortened usually to trading. The chaps taking part were known as traders. When the market for one product declined they usually found another in demand. Not that the long-haul routes were the best place for the traders. Rumour had it that there were great opportunities in Europe. It was, of course, well known that the Germans had carted off vast quantities of treasure from the occupied countries, and a great deal of it was 'liberated' again, in turn, by the occupying armies and, more particularly, by the various government agencies and commissions set up to settle the country. Anyone involved in the provision of transport in this situation found their services much in demand. On the eastern routes, although there was no such major activity, a lively trade sprang up in such diverse things as watches, shoes, sunglasses, carpets and tea. The tea trade was the most profitable. A one-pound packet of tea, readily available for about two shillings in India, fetched a pound in Egypt. A spare suitcase filled with tea produced a profit of nearly £20, a not inconsiderable sum at the time. Unknown to the crews, the ground staff began to take a hand, filling crates marked 'Stores' with tea for their opposite numbers to sell in Cairo.

One chap I knew, we'll call him 'Trader', latched on to this traffic and quickly progressed from the spare suitcase level to suitably disguised consignments of 2,000 pounds a time. The laws of supply and demand quickly began to take effect as the Egyptians found their favourite beverage more readily available again and the price began to drop sharply. My trader friend confided in me afterwards that it was more than the law of supply and demand that was involved. The Special Investigation Branch got interested and lay in wait for the next unfortunate to arrive at Almaza. Somehow Trader got wind of this. In vain is the trap laid in sight of the bird.

Stories were spread of a York circling over the Canal Zone with the crew shovelling Orange Pekoe down the flare chute, for all the world as they had shovelled out leaflets over Germany not so long before. There may be no truth in this: stories told around the bar are notoriously unreliable.

I met Trader one day in the Mess. 'Trader', I said, 'I've missed you down the routes. What are you doing with yourself these days?' The authorities, he complained, had somehow, and quite unjustifiably, thought he had got involved in the Cairo tea swindle. Although there wasn't a shred of evidence to support this, they'd taken him off route flying for the time being. He offered me a lift to London and I accepted. It was a struggle to get into the passenger seat of his car. It was jammed with stuff. 'Trader', I said, 'what is all this stuff?'. He had been put in charge of the POW labour, he told me. 'Marvellous blokes they were, spent all their spare time making things'. 'What sort of things?' I asked him, trying to make a little more room for myself. 'Toys mostly', he replied. 'It may have escaped your notice, but there's a great shortage of toys and the festive season's not far off. I've been trying to help them find the materials they need, paint and wood and the like and I've taken over disposing of the stuff for them. Just think of all those kids waking up on Christmas morning and finding a lovely rocking horse in their stocking'.

I thought about it, the bright-eyed children, the industrious prisoners longing for home and so profitably employed, and my friend liberating all the materials necessary for such a worthy purpose and making it all possible. The authorities couldn't have found a better man. 'Trader', I said, 'I expect you'll wind up a millionaire, if you keep out of jail'. 'Flying', he said, 'is for the birds'. We drove into London in companionable silence.

Other people were beginning to think of demob and what lay beyond. Some had managed to get seconded to the British Overseas Airways Corporation (BOAC) as the civilian airlines were struggling back into business and beginning to expand. Because of my age and lack of seniority, my demob date lay well ahead, but I began to think of how to turn all this route experience to account. I therefore made a start on getting my pilot's B licence.

Towards the end of 1946 I had begun the long, hard process of accumulating route experience and a knowledge of climatology, and the particular systems affecting the various regions between Europe and Singapore. It was then that I'd had my first brush with the south-west monsoon over India. It has to be remembered that, in those days, we flew unpressurised, without the benefit of weather radar. Terminal and en route weather had to be taken into account for a safe operation, and delaying and cancelling flights when the forecasts were adverse were the main methods by which we sought to avoid the worst conditions. Transport Command were becoming highly organised in testing and categorising their crews and initiated a system of card holders. This card system worked well enough coming into the UK where, in the face of adverse conditions, group would signal, 'Green card holders only'. While the white card holders then had to stay put, the green card captains were free to operate, but at their own discretion. This system, of course, didn't extend beyond the Mediterranean and we were left to make our own decisions elsewhere. For all those passengers who have been involved in weather delays and diversions over the years, it may be interesting to note that in Britain at least, this area of decision-making has been left to the individual captain.

One day, crossing India bound for Dum Dum Airport at Calcutta, I ran into increasing cloud and heavy, turbulent weather. At first, the base was fairly high and, by descending, we were able to continue in reasonable conditions. As we progressed the base lowered and, because of the terrain safety height, to descend further was out of the question. We bumped and rolled our way through it, no longer able to pick a way around the worst of the turbulent clouds, so I tried a higher level but without improvement. I was reluctant to turn back, knowing what we had already flown through and, ever hopeful of an improvement, continued on. We had a very rough ride tossed about in the cumulonimbus, unable to find the way around, either by going lower because of terrain or much higher because of icing. I was very relieved to reach Dum Dum and find conditions there quite good although ringed about with towering thunderstorms. I thought, as we taxied in and parked on the apron, that people stopped and looked at us curiously. We soon found out why. The centre fin was missing, giving the aircraft a slightly odd appearance. No doubt because of the slab-sided fuselage, A V Roe had given the York a third and centre fin to aid stability. I must say I had been too busy nursing the aeroplane along to notice its departure or to be able to say if it had any effect.

There followed a long delay. Signals flew back and forth to obtain a new fin. It wasn't a common stock item, but eventually, one arrived from the UK and the engineers fitted it. Things are not always as straightforward as they might seem. There was evidence of corrosion around the two fittings so it was reasonable to suppose that the fin was already weak and waiting for the opportunity to break off. The fittings weren't normally visible as it had a fairing riveted around the base, but no fairing had arrived, only the fin itself, and we had no metal bashers capable of making one. I was unable to persuade the engineers that it didn't need a fairing. But without one, they wouldn't sign it out. Eventually, as the delay dragged on, I managed to persuade them to improvise. They fitted the gap at the bottom of the fin with yards and yards of fabric liberally covered in dope and, when I pronounced it satisfactory, they signed it up and we set off to ferry the aircraft home. All went well until we reached Malta.

As the RAF had a fairly comprehensive maintenance facility at Luqa in Malta they were bound to be interested. Unknown to us, on the last sector into Malta, the dope had given up and the fabric started to unwind and so, once again, we ground to a halt, or very nearly. Before they could get into the signals exchange and the hunt for a non-existent fairing, I managed to persuade the ground crew chief to remove the remains of the fabric and convinced him that the thing would fly without a fairing or indeed, without a fin. Every now and again, you come across chaps whose lives are ruled by common sense, who have sufficient confidence and robustness of outlook to be able to interpret the rules for themselves and not be bound hand and foot by them. In Malta I had met such a one. We were signed up and on our way the next day without the fabric or further hindrance. I had expected that searching enquiry would be made on my return but nothing happened. I think the dread word, corrosion, had set them scurrying in other directions.

Towards the end of the year I was posted from Number 511 Squadron to Number 51 at Waterbeach, near Cambridge. They had been flying Liberators and, having lost those with the end of lease-lend, had re-equipped with Yorks. Those of us who were sent there liked to think we had been sent to provide a nucleus of experience, but wisely refrained from voicing any such opinions. We continued to operate the same routes with much the same mix of passengers, mail and freight. One or two changes were introduced, some stemming from civilian airline procedures and others from a shift back to RAF peacetime practice. The crew concept was abandoned and individuals were rostered to form a crew for a particular flight or series of flights. We became aware that we were expected to take a more active part in the life of the mess and the station, to the extent of joining the station parades. Heretofore, after a trip, when the monthly stint of training flights were completed, it had been accepted that we could disappear until next required for service. I became uneasily aware that the 'old order changeth'.

We had another York squadron next door, involved mainly in

VIP flights and specials of one sort or another. Once or twice, finding themselves otherwise engaged, they ceded some of these to Number 51, and so it was that I got involved briefly in the VIP business. My experience at this time was enough to teach me that I wasn't cut out for the role of VIP pilot. It requires a particular sort of chap.

We were sent out to Singapore as a temporary replacement for the Supremo's regular crew and aircraft. It would be about six weeks, they said. The first snag with VIP work soon became apparent. You spend a lot of time hanging about, awaiting the summons to go where ever needed, generally at very short notice, as a sort of permanent stand-by. We did a flight to Delhi and, after a day or two, returned to Changi in Singapore. Then there was a flap. The Supremo had to attend a function in the UK. I confess, I was a bit disappointed when, as if by magic, his regular crew appeared with a shining aircraft. We were to act as backup and bring the baggage and any staff left over.

On the way into Malta, one of the engines packed up. I decided it would have to be changed and entered it up in the log as unserviceable. Then I hit the next snag with VIP work: delays are not acceptable and there was a bit of a fuss. I couldn't see the problem. The VIP aeroplane had got away all right and we had only the baggage. But that *was* the problem, apparently. I had no wish to cause the great man embarrassment on parade with just what he stood up in, but at the same time, I didn't want to get ahead of my time with engine-out ferry flights. The engine was changed and, when all was ready, we set forth again for the final stage.

Shortly after our return to base, I was summoned to Group Headquarters, Such a summons usually indicated only one thing. I was to appear at a stated hour the next day. Transport was to be laid on by the M T section. It must be quite serious. I knew I was fireproof, so I lost no sleep over it. On the next morning however, I dressed with care, checking to see that the wire stiffener was still in my hat and my shoes were polished. My trousers had responded well to being under the mattress and altogether, I was satisfied with my appearance. I waited close by the front door of the officers' mess for the transport. I wondered if they'd send a Humber, one of those staff cars with the big balloon tyres and roundels painted on the sides and a flag holder carefully covered over up front. A motor bike and side-car made its way up to the front door. I could hardly believe it. The driver was apologetic. It was the best they could do at such short notice. He began to turn the argument round so that it seemed my fault. I glanced anxiously at the sky, heavy with rain clouds, and then at the side-car. The driver helped me to install myself in the side-car. It was my first experience of such a thing. We set off. I regaled myself with, 'Doctor Foster went to Gloucester, in a shower of rain'.

The skies opened. I considered myself better placed than the driver until I remembered that he didn't have to undergo any kind of inspection on arrival. I cowered down inside my cubicle. The engine barked away cheerfully by my right ear. I began to imagine that it was missing a beat occasionally. After a little while it became apparent that it wasn't just imagination. Then it started misfiring badly and we were losing power. We came to a halt by a muddy roadside in what seemed to me the middle of nowhere. The rain seemed to have eased a bit now that our forward progress had ceased.

I made inquiry of the driver as to the cause of our misfortune. It became clear that the mechanics of the thing were a mystery to him. I asked if there were any tools. There were, and he produced them. We agreed to start on the fuel system, which had given every indication of an engine running out of fuel. As there was plenty in the tank, it pointed to a carburettor problem. Starting most carefully, I set about dismantling the wretched thing. Needless to say, once engrossed in such a task, with time pressing, the priorities change and motor bikes are oily, dirty things at best. Carburettors are delicate and fiddly and have to be dismantled and reassembled with care. I cast about me for something to accept the parts. Nothing offered except my hat. I laid it carefully beside me and laid each part within. Eventually, with the carburettor cleared of dirt and water and after kicking over a few times, the engine sprang back into life. We continued on our way. I should have chucked it then but I have a streak of determination, so we continued grimly on. There was no time to restore my appearance. I looked ruefully at my hat. I had only one glove. I must have cut a sorry figure. I was ushered straight into the presence by an anxious NCO.

In matters of law, I believe, ignorance is no excuse. Equally, in the matter of appointments with senior officers there is no excuse for being late or dishevelled and my attempted apologies were abruptly dismissed. In the matter of VIP flights, delays are inexcusable. I quickly tired of trying to state my case and fell silent. His brief, evidently, was to give me a rollicking and he was not to be diverted or confounded by the facts. I don't think he'd really noticed my appearance at first, it only got to him gradually. I thought he might have apoplexy. When he'd finished, I was dismissed and left.

I set off to find the MT driver. There was no sign of him. I found the motor bike. Just as I was kicking the thing over to get it started, he reappeared, anxious to drive me back. He seemed to be under the impression that I might well have gone without him. In that, he was dead right. I don't remember the drive back. My hat was never the same again. I had it cleaned and chucked the wire away.

Despite my unpromising start, I was shortly given another 'special'. One of the wartime aces was to attempt a new record from the UK to Cape Town, flying in a Mosquito. My part in this was to distribute spare parts and ground crew at his scheduled landing places and diversionary fields. Loaded up with Mosquito bits and pieces and ground crew, we set off in our York from the UK and duly delivered the personnel and spares as far as Kisumu on the northern shores of Lake Victoria. At this point we had an engine failure and we were unable to continue to the Cape. We waited there for yet another York to appear to take over and to bring us a serviceable engine. Meantime, the record breaking attempt went ahead to a successful conclusion.[3] We

3 In 1947 Squadron Leader H B 'Micky' Martin, of Dambuster fame, flew a Mosquito from London to Cape Town in the record time of 21 hours 30 minutes.

saw nothing of him as he either transited Kisumu in the night or overflew it. The local populace took us to their hearts and made us very welcome at the hotel. My co-pilot was a keen sportsman and games player and he accepted an invitation to play in a friendly match with the local soccer team. A good time was had by all, but there was an unfortunate outcome. Although it was a friendly game, Jock got his leg broken. He was taken to hospital where the medical officer set his leg in plaster and the staff made a fuss of him.

By this time, the replacement engine had arrived and preparations for our departure were well advanced. Although no good purpose would have been served in continuing to the Cape, I had signalled to base my intention to do so, in the faint hope that doing so might go unnoticed and thus receive tacit approval. I was instructed to return, collecting the spare parts and bodies en route as soon as we were serviceable. I pondered how best to break the news of a further delay. My co-pilot was anxious not to be left behind in Africa and he and the medical officer hatched a plan between them. The medical friend, lately released from the army, had cast his lot with the Colonial service. He had come to the conclusion that he'd made a mistake, but breaking his contract would have involved him in the expense of a return fare and here was an opportunity to escort a patient back to UK and solve his dilemma in one move. Jock declared himself perfectly fit for duty, if hampered slightly by his broken leg, but he could put the gear up and down at my behest and generally make himself useful. It seemed to me to be all perfectly practical, although unlikely to meet official approval and, to save time, I didn't put the arrangement to the test. So that's what we did and we made our way back, retracing our steps and collecting up the spare bits and bodies.

Only one incident arose to mar the return flight or make it in any way memorable. On the way into Khartoum from the south, we were cleared for a straight in approach and given number one to land. I slowed the aeroplane and made all ready in good time. This threw the ETA out by a few minutes and

Author (centre) and crew members before an Avro York.

put the controller in a slight quandary. He had other traffic, a civilian airliner, approaching from the north and it soon appeared that he would arrive overhead first and be forced to delay before landing. Very wisely, in my opinion, the controller stuck to his plan and we continued to land as number one. The civil flight made a circuit and followed us in but so arranged his affairs that he got too close and had to overshoot at a late stage while we were still occupying the runway. I made my way upstairs to the control tower to report and file a flight plan for the next stage to Wadi Haifa. Presently I was joined by the civilian captain and two of his crew. He was an impressive figure of immense age and great seniority, judging by the amount of gold braid he carried. He was also in high dudgeon. His crew, on the other hand, hung back sheepishly. He started in on both myself and the controller.

I was quite prepared, to start with, to offer my apologies for not revising my ETA and having discommoded him, but after a while, I tired of his tirade. He got to threatening to report the incident to whatever authorities govern such matters in both the Sudan and London. 'Methinks he doth protest too much', I thought. Having got himself upset in this way, it seemed likely that he'd gone on to cock up his next approach and landing and someone had to suffer for it. I made it plain that I couldn't accept any responsibility if he so mismanaged his affairs and advised him to go ahead and report it and make an even bigger ass of himself if he so wished.

As I walked back across the tarmac, I reflected sadly on the matter. If I did join the civil airlines, I might have to fly with chaps like that, or worse, with that particular chap. Another and more distressing thought occurred. Maybe with time and age, I myself might grow to be like that. I climbed back on the aeroplane and banished the thought.

On the last sector over France we received a signal to divert to Manston for customs clearance. I saw nothing untoward in this. Probably our arrival time was inconvenient for the local customs staff but I knew, from previous experience, that Manston customs were sticklers and might well be upset by anything unorthodox in our complement. The big snag was the doctor's baggage. When we were in Kisumu he hadn't emphasised the fact that he intended taking all his worldly possessions with him, ex-army crates containing medical books and gear, but also all manner of personal things, including his wartime souvenirs and his ex-service revolver. I called the good doctor forward to the flight deck and told him the news. I explained that I would have to take charge of his boxes and the keys as they were now unlikely to be mistaken for Mosquito spare parts. He himself would have to be less noticeable and try to shed his 'pongo' look. Transport Command had, by this time, solved the problem of unsuitable clothing by issuing lightweight flying suits. It happened that we had a spare. There was nothing critical about the fit, it was an all-enveloping type of garment.

I wasn't disappointed in customs. They wanted to see everything. I explained my embarrassment about the boxes. I'd been lumbered by this medical chum of mine. I owed him a favour and he'd asked me if I'd take some kit home for him. It had turned out to be more than I'd expected. He'd assured me it was all medical gear and did they want to see it? They did. The senior customs officer pointed to one of the boxes. 'That one', he said. I fumbled with the keys. 'Here, let me do that for you skipper', said the Doc. He unlocked the box and flung it open. It was full of medical books. The customs man got busy with his chalk and we loaded everything back on board and proceeded to base. There the doctor took his leave of us to make his apologies to his employers and make a fresh start. Jock's leg mended without further trouble and, as far as I know, was as good as new.

As the date approached for my demob, I tucked my shining new B licence, along with an application form for the second class navigation licence into the back of my logbook and started on the rounds of the airlines. This was a quite different sort of feeing market. The small, short-haul outfits were being rounded up to become part of the new British European Airways (BEA) and the prospects there seemed uncertain. Continental airlines were still recruiting, particularly the Scandinavians. British South American Airways (BSAA) had been formed and consisted really of Bennett and his Pathfinders, thinly disguised. I went along for an interview and was offered a job as a first officer, but there was a catch to it. First officers were to take over the navigation and had to be qualified and licensed. I'd had a look through the first-class navigators' syllabus and found it daunting.

With one offer open, I tried BOAC. I'd come too late for a direct command but, subject to meeting their medical requirements, I was offered a first officer's contract with a good prospect of early promotion. On this latter point, the selection board were slightly out of touch. The medics set me a problem. Not the old one about touching toes. They didn't like my nose. I had what they called a deflected septum and they were of the opinion that I should have it straightened before I could be accepted. I went back to the RAF to see if they could oblige me with a minor operation and got as far as an ear, nose and throat specialist. 'Rubbish', he said, 'absolute rubbish, have no part of it!' I reported back to the BOAC medical department with the specialist's opinion, suitably rephrased. As they saw it, this was one medical opinion against another and they had the say.

The author at the controls of an RAF Avro York.

Although I am not a betting man, I had a suggestion. Just down the road was a large London hospital, no doubt equipped with an ENT department and specialists. Was it possible to obtain a third opinion and, whichever way it went, could we agree to abide by it? Rather to my surprise they went along with the idea and made a couple of phone calls, and I trotted along to the hospital. The specialist had a quick shufti and asked a question or two. I mentioned the RAF chap and fortunately remembered his name. That clinched it. He came down on the side of his RAF colleague. I rather thought he might, although I'd not have wagered too much on it. They made out a 'fit' report rather grudgingly, I thought, and added some unfavourable remarks about a poor long-term health risk. In that they turned out to be wrong, I'm happy to say, but in fact, I revised my opinion of the Corp-oration's medics over the years and, although I had very little need of their professional services, I found them absolutely first rate. One particular doctor, Alan Sibbald, became something of a legend in his own time and was a firm favourite with all the flight crew who came within his orbit.

Weighing it up, I thought BOAC had the edge. They didn't at that time foresee any requirement for me to navigate their aeroplanes, so I accepted their offer. I still have the original agreement for service, a handsome document printed on high-quality paper, setting out the pay and conditions. My starting salary was £600 per annum, a princely sum by the standards of that time. The basic pay scales had just been altered, the printed list crossed out and marked cancelled and a typewritten list attached to the document. Senior captains (first class) had been raised from a flat rate of £1,100 per annum to £1,500 with annual increments, to a maximum of £1,650. Despite the ravages of inflation and the debasement of our currency, today's senior captain who is pulling down in excess of £30,000 a year[4] probably still feels that there are times when he earns it, and more. I'm not so sure.

When I had completed a couple more trips, some further BABs training and a series of air tests, the time came to proceed to Blackpool where they were handing out the demob suits. When I came out laden with all this new gear, the spivs were missing and no one offered me money for it. My Uncle Jock thought he might be able to dispose of it and he got a good price for the mackintosh, but the suit had to be given away. I suspected that they were still employing the same bunch of tailors, now trying their hand at civilian clothing.

And so I set forth to try my hand at civilian flying with 2,182 hours, fifteen minutes behind me and a brand new logbook costing six shillings and sixpence (plus purchase tax) bought from HM Stationery Office, in company with all the other likely lads who had lately 'beaten their swords into ploughshares.'

In my case, however, I wanted no part of ploughshares, having experienced the real thing and found them not to my liking.

---

4 Written in 1982.

The long apprenticeship

My introduction to the airline was via Aldermaston. The overseas and European Corporations had got together and set up a combined training establishment there. Although I was fully qualified and licensed on the York aircraft, I still had to make up the numbers and go through the complete technical course. This made for a nice easy start, as the systems and flying side were already familiar to me and only various minor changes in operating procedures had to be studied.

The winter weather of 1946–1947 turned severe and austerity Britain became even more austere as a result. We were, however, comfortable enough in camp and, apart from one experiment by the canteen staff with whale meat steaks, which were largely left uneaten, to be served up again over the next few days in various guises like rissoles, it was an enjoyable start. My own plans to marry were all going ahead and my bride-to-be had moved to a job in nearby Reading so we were able to meet frequently. Just how we had met on a Transport Command flight is a romantic story that I have been instructed not to retell as having no place in this narrative.

At the end of the training period, the office staff submitted my name for the Air Registration Board (ARB) examination and, as I had already qualified, I didn't attend. It took quite a bit of sorting out and I must have failed to convince them as they straight away arranged a further examination. By the time this was due I had left Aldermaston to proceed to Hurn near Bournemouth, which was the York fleet operational base at that time. There was some disturbing news from BEA, which had decided that they had overdone the recruitment of pilots and laid off sixty or so who were still undergoing their initial training. Their hopes of a career in aviation had been quickly dashed. Over the next two years, however, a reconsideration of their crewing requirements led to their efforts to locate the redundant chaps and to rehire them. Neither Corporation was very successful in predicting the level of business they would attract and hence their manning requirements, so their crystal ball remained cloudy and the aviation business, although growing mightily, remained very cyclic in nature. The experiment in co-operation between the sister airlines by offering a combined training unit did not last. When the immediate post-war bulge of recruits had been absorbed into the business, it was closed down.

The Hurn base was yet another hutted camp situated in the midst of heath on the edge of the New Forest. The Corporation's business was divided up into lines. Number Two line was based at Hurn. These lines and bases were scattered about the world. Number One line had been mainly Dakotas (DC3's), based at Whitchurch, near Bristol and that had been sacrificed to form the nucleus of BEA. Number One line pilots had the option of remaining with their beloved Daks or transferring to another line in BOAC. A small number had transferred to the Yorks and were readily distinguishable from their fellows in that, given the opportunity, they were loud in their lamentations for happier, bygone days.

The pride, and the envy, of the entire company was Number Three line. They flew the Atlantic routes and were based in Montreal, which sounded very romantic and exciting from austerity Britain. Even more exciting was the extra pay and allowances that the North Atlantic route attracted. I'm still rather vague about Number Four line. I think it must have been concerned with flying boats, and Number Five line was even more of a mystery, being located in Cairo and operating a variety of curious aeroplanes.

In addition to this scattered collection of 'air-lines', the British had somehow acquired a multitude of smaller airlines, later known as associated companies. These operated within their own patch from the West Indies to the Far East. Never was there a nation better placed to exploit and develop civil aviation than the British, for various reasons.

To start with. there was a surplus of wartime pilots of

considerable experience competing for the available jobs. The civil aviation authorities of that time had to hire great halls as examination rooms to accommodate the candidates undergoing licence examinations and aviation schools sprang up to cater for them and coach them through the various syllabuses. A huge aircraft manufacturing industry had emerged after the war, which was ready to turn to the manufacture of civil aeroplanes although, such had been their concentration on military machines that they were woefully short of suitable designs, having left this to the US manufacturers. But the world airline routes had been pioneered before the war and kept alive and further developed by both the North Atlantic ferry service and the Empire air services, which BOAC had struggled to maintain throughout.

It seemed to me then that a great and glorious prospect opened up before us. I guess I was young and buoyed up by youthful hopes and optimism and, moreover, I had been part of an air force that had put great armadas of aeroplanes into the air and everything seemed possible. The reality, however, was very different. Shortages and rationing were the order of the day and Britain had become timid and inclined to a form of socialism, making a priority of fair shares for all and with little thought for restoring the national wealth so that there would be something worth sharing.

The Yorks served the African and eastern routes, all fairly familiar to me, and converted Lancasters, known as Lancastrians, were employed for the long-haul to Australia. Although the Lancastrians were hardly suitable as airliners, seating only twelve passengers, some of whom had to clamber over the main spar to reach their seats, they were hailed as a considerable success in cutting the time to Sydney. 'Three dawns to Sydney' was the boast taken from the title of a publicity film made at that time.

I set about learning to be a good co-pilot. There were times, I must admit, when I found it hard, particularly when flying with captains of my own generation, whose experience was little greater than my own and, in many cases, had done far less on the aircraft type. I put such thoughts firmly behind me. I was fortunate to have a good job in aviation in a premier company and I had a lot to learn. There is no substitute for a sound apprenticeship and no better way of learning than from following good examples and having experience.

Number Two line was staffed mainly by ex-RAF pilots with a sprinkling of experienced pre-war pilots. The management seemed an odd lot. Some were pre-war pilots who had forsaken flying to become full-time administrators. Others were from various ground trades or had been administrators in the RAF. I had been accustomed to being part of a very tight-knit unit, an operational squadron or a training unit and this was very different. The aircrews led a separate existence, being rostered for flights and standing down at home, with little contact at base apart from check flights and occasional stand-by duties at the airport. There was a quite remarkable lack of contact between the flying and the ground staff; a feature of civil aviation that is as marked in the 1980s as it was in the 1940s.

The management endeavoured to keep in touch by issuing notices. These varied from a range of aviation subjects to the more mundane matters of behaviour and deportment. These orders were a strange blend of civilian and military, usually ending with the words, 'Severe disciplinary action will be taken'. I was unclear as to whether the managers deliberately added the threats at the end from long habit or whether the office staff, equally from habit, added them in an attempt to round off the notice. There was a further complication for me. At about the same time, the Corporation had hired three of us with the surname Gray, all co-pilots and, although one Gray, my friend from the Transport Command days, wasn't on Number Two line, the management seemed to have us confused, imagining that they had only one Gray, not three. If one of the others got into a scrape, and they did seem prone to it, I was sent for. It should have worked the other way round as well, but I don't think it did. My namesake had got into some kind of difficulty in Karachi and a report had come back to base. I was summoned to the fleet manager's office.

I forget how my summons came. I set off, however, on my bicycle from home in the New Forest and, not knowing the reason for the summons, took along my briefcase containing my flying logbook on the pillion. This was just as well. I was ushered into the great man's presence and stood, ill at ease, while he rapidly recounted the details of my alleged misdemeanours. The name Karachi struck me. I interrupted to ask when it had happened. Somewhat impatiently he told me the date. I produced my logbook. On the date in question I had been in Johannesburg. It was a complete stopper. He was not only mystified but very cross. I made no attempt to enlighten him. It really didn't occur to me that he could be so ignorant of his staff. I regret to say that he made no attempt to apologise for his error and I left his office to cycle home, with the unhappy feeling that somehow this silly episode epitomised the entire relationship between air and ground staff. Now, many years on, despite changes in management structure and circumstances, this incident still illustrates the gap between aircrew and ground staff and it may be one of the root causes of Britain's unhappy industrial record.

We talked of flying as 'going down the line' or 'down the routes'. Number Two line had a splendid selection of flights. There was, perhaps the least popular, the route to Lagos and Accra. I rather liked it because the trips were short and there was no east–west time change. The first slip, or lay-over, was Tripoli. The airport, Castel Benito, was named after the Italian dictator, linking Libya with the days of Italian influence and dominance. The Company's offices were located within one of the hangars previously occupied by the passenger and freight staff of Transport Command. I never failed to notice the shell and bullet holes that punctured the great doors and walls of the building. In the early days we lived in the old military accommodation nearby, driving to reach the mess through a splendid archway adorned with eagles that was bequeathed by Benito. Later, when we moved to hotel accommodation in the town, I found Tripoli to be a pleasant, indeed beautiful spot, although the harbour was still cluttered with sunken ships and the signs of the recent war were everywhere evident. The place then was very poor and down at heel, but wine production had been restarted and the local vintage 'Ruberaffa' was readily available, although it was often bottled in old beer bottles or other unlikely containers. The wine waiters carried beer bottle cap removers, not corkscrews.

The hotel we used was a delightful blend of Italian fittings and decor, with Arab courtyards and gardens linking the various buildings. The rooms were small, full of dark wood, with cupboard doors which, when opened, took up all the available space; and the rooms were linked in pairs by a sort of miniature bathroom comprising, on one side a sit-up bathtub and, on the other, a usually smelly urinal. The plumbing was Italian in style and Arabic in execution; a most undesirable combination. It made a unique home from home. The staff were very friendly and could produce the finest spaghetti or cannelloni I have ever sampled. Indeed, I feel they may have led me adrift here, as the genuine article served in Italy seems a poor dish in comparison with that concocted by their exiled cousins in Tripoli.

The route across the great Sahara desert to Nigeria was, of course, flown at night for good navigation reasons. For most of the year, apart from occasions when high over running cirrus made life difficult, we used astronavigation and we carried, as part of the regular crew, a specialist navigator, along with a radio officer for long-distance communication. One of the navigator's first tasks, when we had picked up the outbound heading and, as the radio beacon faded behind us and became unreliable, was to set up his sextant and make a course check. Once happy that the compasses were accurate and the pilots had settled on the correct heading, he would open his air almanac and plan his first astro fix for just after top of climb.

The aviators had adapted the methods of the mariners to suit their particular environment. When there was no sea horizon, an air bubble floating in the sextant was substituted and for each sight a large number of shots were taken by the sextant and averaged over a run of two minutes. The calculations were made beforehand from precomputed tables. With the observed readings noted between shots and adjusted for the time lapse, the position could be fixed very quickly after the final shot was completed. The air plot position, when joined to the fix, gave the wind and, if needed, a course correction was handed up to the pilots and the detailed position report made to the radio officer for transmission to the appropriate control centre. Provided the pilots attended carefully to their flying during the period of the shooting, those skilled navigators could keep close to the track with every confidence. As the dawn lightened the sky, Kano would lie directly ahead right on ETA.

The weather in West Africa is very seasonal. In summer the moist and cloudy conditions of the coast move north, drawn by the low heat of the desert interior, and large thunderstorm clouds develop, reaching to Kano and beyond. In winter, when the pressure pattern is reversed, the outflow of air from the desert reaches down to the coast, bringing the Harmattan (the doctor), and dust-laden winds to northern Nigeria. So there were times when a beacon let-down was necessary at Kano and, if you were caught out by really poor visibility, a diversion had to be made to Lagos.

Now and again we met up with the local pilots who were flying for West African Airways. They were mostly British and some of them were originally first officers with the main line BOAC who had tired of being long-term co-pilots and had transferred to the associated companies to command smaller aeroplanes. When they were established as captains, they planned to return to BOAC and keep their rank. Eventually some of them did, in fact, do this, and good luck to them, but as the more vocal first officers made their voices heard back at base so their association moved to head off this particular form of short cut. But, at the time, little of this was evident and the chaps we met were good company and made us welcome in their houses. In many ways they had done well in return for the lot of an exile, with company houses and furniture, imported motor cars bought free of taxes, often with money loaned to them by their employer, and a good many such perks not open to their UK-based colleagues. I confess that I didn't envy them, as the same choice was open to me and I had decided against it. I kept in touch, however, with one particular friend there who had been with me on the course at Aldermaston.

In Lagos an assured welcome awaited us. The Ikeja Arms

Hotel was run by a great character, Joe Harold, known and liked by all the aircrew. We were made to feel most welcome in his establishment. Joe was also well known and liked by the people in Lagos and was eventually honoured by being made a chief. For a white man in the rising tide of anti-colonialism this was no mean achievement. If Joe was made a West African chief, he was also, to my mind, a chief among hotel-keepers. On seeing a group of crew members seated in his lounge, he would make his way over to them and ensure that they were plentifully supplied with liquid refreshment, usually in the form of a tray full of large green bottles of Carlsberg. At some point, he would turn the conversation to the question of dinner and a menu would appear, but Joe's main interest was to see you had something you liked, whether it was on the menu or not. Joe's curried prawns were unsurpassed, but it was the side dishes and condiments that made the dish memorable. A chieftain among curries without a doubt. As Joe prospered, his establishment grew and the standard of creature comfort improved. Eventually he went on to add an Olympic-sized swimming pool and even a casino.

The route also served Accra and, as it was the terminal point for most of the services, we had more time there. This was time to visit the beach, to bathe, or attempt to, in the dangerous surf and picnic on pineapples and coconuts sold by seaside vendors. At first, before the advent of international hotels, our accommodation was in local bashas. Toilet facilities were provided by way of thunder boxes. These were rather open-air affairs, constructed of solid planks of West African mahogany and it was as well to know just when they were due to be emptied. Many a morning constitutional was rudely interrupted by the arrival of the 'honey cart' when the trap door would be flung open and the bucket disappear at a most critical time.

The laundry service was also of a very high repute. A bundle of laundry, whatever its composition, cost sixpence and was returned all steaming and warm from the ironing that self-same evening.

One of the captains, and a great favourite of mine was Charles Rowe (God rest his soul). Charlie had a reputation for being close with his money, although he was a man of generous good nature in all else. I often suspected that he took great amusement in the stories of his meanness and did things to cultivate this impression. Thus, one morning, shortly after my arrival, he popped his head around my door to ask if I was sending laundry. 'Yes, Charlie', I replied, 'I'm just setting out a little bundle now'. Charlie, it transpired, had thought it would be a good idea if we combined bundles as, in that way, we could each save threepence. I was quite agreeable. But there was a snag. Charlie had only brought two shirts and I had more than that. He pointed out that it wouldn't be even and appeared perplexed as how best to make it even. Then, just as he had anticipated, to save further bother, I agreed to put his shirts in my bundle and hang the expense. Charlie went away chortling, and so did I, as I had acquired another neat little story to add to my collection about him and so enhance his reputation further.

On the return trip from the Coast we arrived back to rationed Britain, usually with a few large green pineapples which, if well chosen for their state of ripeness, would survive the journey and, if not, with their insides rotten, would enhance any compost heap. I particularly favoured the guinea fowl eggs from Kano. If I had arranged it beforehand, these would be waiting for collection on the way back and, being very hard shelled, travelled well and did a great deal to supplement the rations and food shortages of the time.

Stories went around that Charlie had most of his furniture made out there and shipped it back to the UK a piece at a time. If so, Charlie wasn't the only one. Along with a good many other things that had become the casualties of peacetime was good quality timber. The stuff used to make the utility furniture available on 'dockets' in the UK was only fit to make packing cases. But this story about Charlie wasn't true. To buy ready-made furniture would have been very extravagant. What he did was carefully choose and buy timber planks that fitted easily in the holds and he made the furniture himself, and very sound and good stuff it was.

The most popular route, certainly to me, was from the UK to

East and South Africa. Again, lasting about a week to ten days or so, depending on the itinerary and frequency of services, it was just about the right length of time to be away from home and, just as important, about the right length of time to share with a small company of men. It was long enough to get to know each other and enjoy the company, yet not too long to tire of the others or become bored. If you were unfortunate enough to have a difficult captain or were merely incompatible with him in some respect, it was not too long to be able to endure while maintaining civilities. Again with no significant time zone change, covering interesting and civilised places and no great weather problems, it was a route I invariably enjoyed.

But the Yorks were not popular on the route, as they had recently supplanted the flying boats. From what we were told, that was the way to fly and, with their passing, the era of civilised travel had ended. Although I never experienced it, I was prepared to believe it. It would have been preferable to arrive on cool waters with a slight splash, instead of a hot bumpy runway, to be taken ashore for the night to an agreeable hostelry and the pleasant company of like-minded people, instead of a grubby transit lounge for an hour of boredom, to arrive at destination refreshed instead of tired and crumpled after long confinement in a cramped and noisy cabin.

We endured the comparisons as best we could. What the York had to offer, like all land planes, was speed and convenience, which is what air travel is about and has increasingly become so. That is not to say that the British were right to abandon the flying boat so readily, and their advocates still maintain that they had a great potential and future. But the nations of the world were ready to create large airports and lay miles of concrete for the land planes, robbing the boats of their natural advantage, together with the harbours and suitable waterways at most of the world's large centres of population.

The Yorks rattled their noisy way up and down the route with a fair degree of reliability and regularity. What gave each trip its own particular flavour and identity depended chiefly upon the nature and personality of the captain. As with any other group of people, captains varied tremendously. Some did their best to turn every trip into an occasion; a triumphal progression. Others saw it as a routine job of work to be got on with. Some took it upon themselves to be disciplinarians. Each one, while bringing to the job his best level of competence and professional skill, varied in outlook and approach and succeeded or failed accordingly in welding together the individual crew members.

While on the trip, we lived and worked in very close proximity and harmony. I'm sure that when this succeeds and a crew works well together it reflects in their entire operation and somehow reflects back on the passengers, who may never see them, but are merely aware that they are there, and have every confidence that they are in good hands.

At the time, fresh from the RAF, I was surprised by some aspects of our life together. There was an astonishing amount of tittle-tattle and bitchiness when people, particularly captains, were discussed. As the job was fairly new and although the pioneering days long over, it was evident that many people, even those doing it, didn't see it as a real job. 'Beats work', they used to say. Either I got used to the cattiness or it died away. Certainly it was a long time before a career in flying became an accepted profession, either by the general public or the aircrew themselves.

We were creatures of habit. Whatever the slip station, be it Cairo or Khartoum or Nairobi, our lives were limited to a particular hotel or rest house and its close environs. Certain clubs or bars became our favourite and it was unusual to venture far beyond the beaten track. Our lives were governed by the next schedule and the need to sleep, or at least rest, before departure. Working what are now called unsocial hours, the paramount need on arrival was to catch up with sleep and try to arrange for the next rest period before flight. In between, we had to fit in eating and recreation as best we could. Very few hotels are able to meet these odd requirements and, as it turned out, using rest houses designed for the purpose by the Corporation became the favoured policy. Their operation could be tailored more exactly to our needs.

In Cairo, the old Osborne House fitted these requirements exactly. Very spartan and unpretentious, it was hidden away among a warren of streets in Cairo itself. At the end of the street was a small bar, not much more than a shop doorway, which became our meeting place and nearby was a noisy nightclub known to the crews as the Conservative Club. I never knew its real name. Should you wish to go further afield, a shout for a 'garry' would produce a battered Cairo taxi at the door and, after the obligatory haggle over the fare, we might venture as far as the local sports club on Gezira Island. It was not unusual to find that people had been transiting Cairo for years and hadn't got round to visiting the Pyramids or Cairo Museum.

From Cairo we followed the course of the river Nile to Khartoum. There, to start with, we stayed in the Grand Hotel overlooking the Nile. Occasionally we had to stay in the houseboat moored in front of it and, at one time, in railway carriages provided by Sudan Railways. Accommodation was always at a premium in Khartoum until the Company built its own rest house, complete with swimming pool and every facility. One night in the Grand Hotel when it was particularly hot, I decided to emulate the locals and sleep outside on the balcony. I dragged the bed out there and made myself comfortable, awaking to find myself covered in a gritty layer of dust. I had chosen an early summer night when the rain belt from East Africa was well north and the storm clouds form, giving birth to the haboob. With or without the storm clouds, a dark roll-like cloud of dust appears on the horizon, moving up from the south east towards the city, blanketing everything in hot smelly dust and reducing visibility to a few hundred yards. I dusted myself off as best I could and moved back inside to continue my sleep, secure in the knowledge that the next flight due was unlikely to arrive in such conditions.

The high altitude and invigorating climate of East Africa made the morning arrival in Nairobi a delight. There were exceptions, however. Airline schedules can never be made to fit all circumstances. The need to fit them to the best times of departure or arrival at major destinations does occasionally mean that you arrive in transit at the worst possible time. In Nairobi this means early morning, particularly in the period February to May and later through September to December when low stratus forms, shrouding the hills from sight and giving a low cloud base. At the time we used the old airport at Eastleigh and great care was needed on the descent and approach with the primitive equipment that was then available. If the base was too low for comfort and the fuel load was insufficient to wait overhead for the cloud to clear, a diversion to Entebbe was sometimes necessary.

There was one other and quite different delight. Eastleigh employed a female radio operator, in itself a most unusual thing, but this particular lady had the most beautiful speaking voice it is possible to imagine. The female voice carries better on the airwaves than the male and her voice had a nightingale quality. After a long night slog, often out of communication with anyone, it fell upon the ears of the most hardened and stubble-faced airman like an unexpected ray of sunshine.

In those days Nairobi was a hive of activity and revival. European settlers were arriving, or returning to take up farming, by sea and by air. Some brave or foolhardy spirits came overland. The white hunters and their acolytes congregated in the bar and environs of the Norfolk Hotel. The hunting safaris were getting underway again, the shooting was still carried out with rifles. The cameras came later. There was no sign or thought as yet of the more terrible shooting and killings to come.

From Nairobi, heading south to Johannesburg, we could not help but be aware of the immensity and variety of Africa. Aware also, that on arrival in Johannesburg, we had transited the seasons from northern winter into southern summer or vice versa. Crossing the equator was still something of a novelty and was recognised on BOAC routes by issuing signed certificates to the passengers. This was probably an inheritance from the flying boats, who had got it from the mariners. It is now such a commonplace event it does not rate a mention from the flight deck.

The shops in Johannesburg were bustling with shoppers and stocked with a great variety of goods, many of them British made, and were evidence of the rising export of luxury goods from the UK, itself starved of such things. Had I been able to afford it, I'd have liked to re-export many of them but had to be content with the sight of well-stocked shelves. There were curious notices on many of the shop doorways. The door was closed, it said, because of weather conditions, but in fact it was open for business and please enter. This was curious to me because I was ignorant of the existence of the gold mine slag heaps. In dry and windy conditions this powdered rock would blow about, bringing the gritty dust to the city, and hence the shopkeepers' precautions. That this no longer happens is because of the technique developed later, of spraying these deposits with liquid mud, changing their appearance and reducing this nuisance. There were other changes afoot in South Africa. I was in Johannesburg when the votes were being counted in the election that swept the National party into power. Excitement and feeling ran high in the city and the hotel had arranged a board in the lounge giving the results as they came in. My friend, Bert, the radio officer, had occasion to go out that evening and, making his way back; to the hotel, some yobbo tackled him demanding to know what he thought of it. Bert had no views on South African politics and expressed himself bluntly. This led to an exchange of blows and Bert took to his heels before others became involved. He appeared the next day with a beautiful 'shiner'. South African politics seem to have been causing strong reactions ever since and Bert can perhaps claim the unique distinction to be among the very first casualties of apartheid.

Perhaps the least popular route was the Indian and far eastern one. The trips were long, with more weather problems and time zone changes and, before the advent of air conditioning, it was hot and sticky during the northern summer. It had its devotees of course, but generally, among the aircrew, anything east of Dover was held to be undesirable. Some held the view that you had to transit the 'Zone of Inefficiency' stretching through the Middle East and India until you broke out on the far side of this hazard. There was, however, a great deal to see and to do and the Speedbird Sports Club, based upon a small monthly subscription, was a thriving industry supplying sports kit at the various regular ports of call. Generally the more civilised places, which offered a wide range of facilities were the least well equipped and the more backward, such as Bahrain and Karachi, where the crews were forced back on their own resources, became the best organised for sport and games and the fun centres along the route. In Karachi, where both BOAC and KLM had built rest houses intended to accommodate and refresh their passengers on the long haul to 'down under', the crew accommodation, if spartan, was marvellously suited to its purpose, and the staff were devoted to the welfare of the crews, making meals available at all hours. The Australian airline, Qantas, shared the facilities there and, as they were great sports and great sportsmen, a lay-over in Karachi was generally a lively affair. At the airport the great airship hangar stood dark and silent; a mute reminder of the great days of the airship and the ill-fated voyage of the Rl0l. Only the birds used it, finding the cavernous roof an ideal roosting place in the absence of the proud shining monsters for which it had so hopefully been designed.

Singapore marked the end of the route for the Yorks and the old Raffles Hotel, rather shabby and down at heel from its more recent occupiers, made a welcome lay-over. Behind the impressive facade, with its fan-shaped palms and gardens, the planters and their wives were back, ordering tea and other refreshments from the Malay and Chinese waiters in a pale and faded re-enactment of the great days of Empire. One could just about imagine the solitary figure seated on a rattan chair and hidden behind the pot plants and pillars to be Somerset Maugham himself, ordering tiffin or some exotic cocktail, awaiting the first raindrops to fall promptly at four o'clock.

I'm glad they didn't pull the old place down as perhaps they should, for as Singapore boomed and new hotels sprang up everywhere to eclipse the old, the Raffles sank into a state of shabby and reduced gentility. But in the dark and once splendid rooms at the back, the tired aircrew could sink into undisturbed slumber, forgetful of the towering cumulonimbus or 'Sumatras' so recently negotiated down the Straits, or the monsoon rain washing across the airfield, and sleep the sleep of the just.

If circumstance suited, to wake early and breakfast in magnificent style in the dining room, as was the British habit in such a place, was always a pleasure. But if not, it was comforting just to awake in pitch darkness and gather one's scattered thoughts, to peer at one's watch and try to add seven and a half hours and arrive at the local time and decide whether the result was of the P M or A M variety. The bell push would bring a silent-footed room boy, who expressed surprise, whatever the hour, if you desired to order breakfast. Within the shortest space of time, waiters appeared and spread fresh linen on the sitting room table and silently serve mangoes and porridge and kippers in turn, along with the dark coffee that was a feature of the country. While you were thus busy with such a repast, enjoying the brief illusion of leisure and well-being, the bedroom would be cleaned and tidied, equally silently. At length, restored and refreshed, you could open the shutters to see if it was indeed day or night.

Some chaps had their own system of awakening to strange places. Somehow you could reach out and turn on the light, whatever the switching arrangement. This information seemed to come without conscious thought. Then, uncertain of your location, you would prowl around the room to locate the writing paper and materials. This would give the hotel and place name. Armed with this information, all that remained was to recall the time difference from GMT and apply it and thus, be relocated. Those with no such system must have caused a serious loss of confidence at times among hotel switchboard staff and receptionists, if they were driven to telephoning to ask, not just the time and place, but whether it was day or night and even, which day of the week.

It is at the halfway stage on a long trip, when the body and mind somehow relax, that one can make good the sleep deficit outbound and start off back refreshed to repeat the process at home. There were unfortunates who found sleep difficult throughout, gradually becoming more tired as the trip progressed, but were somehow buoyed up throughout by reserves of nervous energy that were sufficient to get them round the route and home again. There were some years to go and several accidents to be endured before limitations on flying and duty hours were reluctantly introduced. The airline pilots fought a long campaign for such safeguards. It is not possible to legislate, of course, for all circumstances, but it has helped tremendously to avoid serious, if usually unintentional abuse.

I am aware that a good many passengers have been adversely affected over the years by flight-time restrictions. If they are rigidly applied, in addition to having to endure delay or disruption, it is tough on the passengers or the other airline staff who have laboured to get all ready to be told that the crew are 'out of flight time'. If they are not rigidly applied, however, the regulations are worthless. Of course, there are airlines and countries where the limitations are not applied or are interpreted loosely. Where violations do have to be reported, the report may not be made, or the times may be 'adjusted' either by the captain or his superiors. Airlines that encourage the rigid application of the rules are at a considerable commercial disadvantage against those which do not. As a passenger, if it happens to you, try to temper your natural annoyance and frustration with the thought that it is, after all, in your own best interest. I know it won't seem like it, but it is a safe bet that, if the outfit you're flying with observes that particular rule, it is likely to observe all the others that are there for your protection. It is, I expect, a safe journey you had in mind when you bought the ticket.

Along with a good many other things in aviation, it is only the tip of the iceberg which shows. That's the bit you and I as passengers stumble on when the flight is delayed. The real safeguard in flight-time limitations, more properly called the 'prevention of fatigue in flight crew' lies in the conditions imposed at the rostering and planning stages. This ensures a safe level of manning for the airlines' services. It can be squeezed by the less scrupulous right up to the limits, even to the point of adjusting the flight schedules by ten or fifteen minutes here and there, to get a maximum duty day out of the crew. A reasonable employer will adjust it the other way to give himself some fat in the system, so that in the event of delays, he has something in hand, even if he loses out on productivity. Provided always that the rostering and planning regulations are met, the limitations serve their major purpose. No great harm or fatigue is likely to occur if, on occasion, they have to be exceeded in practice. The captain is, in fact, permitted to use his discretion within narrow limits.

It is a sad fact of life that, once again, the unscrupulous operator in addition to planning right up to the hilt will lean on the captains to use their discretionary time as of right, so that it is no longer discretionary in fact and then lean on them further to get the flight to its destination. The regulating authority exists to prevent such abuse and, usually, they would do so if only they knew about it. But they have to rely on being told by the captain through the airline. Now, airline captains are no different from any other group of people, it's only in the public mind that they seem braver or different from others in less demanding occupations, and that is only because of the legends and nonsense from the pioneering days and the Boys' Own Paper.

In fact, they are if anything, more susceptible to pressure than most. Their livelihood is more at risk than most. Neglecting any hazard that the job itself may produce, all the regular tests and examinations of their health and proficiency promote an attitude whereby one more threat, implied or open, is taken very seriously and the captain is likely to give in. BOAC were certainly not an outfit to lean on their captains. Indeed, for most of their history they were inclined to do the opposite, allowing great discretion to, and placing considerable reliance upon their captains, stemming from the earliest days when they had to do so of necessity. It is therefore ironic that it required an accident to a BOAC aeroplane while landing in Singapore to act as a catalyst for the introduction of flight-time limitations for UK-registered aircraft. In this accident, fatigue was held to be a contributory factor. Such changes are, generally, hard won; and are very often only the result of several aircraft accidents. It is said by the cynical that it requires a minimum of three fatal accidents to produce a change in procedures by the regulating authorities.

It was on a York flight to Nairobi that another, apparently insignificant, change took place. One of the cabin crew members was a stewardess. She was rostered for the flight to act as Auntie to a group of schoolchildren travelling unaccompanied to East Africa. She was the first stewardess I had met. I noticed, straight away, that her presence made a difference to the entire crew. An entirely male group behaves in a particular way and the addition of female company at once modifies this. At that time, at least where male crew members were careless of their language, the swearing stopped when the stewardess appeared. In other and more subtle ways each crew member altered. A pot of tea delivered to the flight deck became the subject of remarks, 'Jolly nice', and 'how very kind'. When the lady departed leaving behind the faint trace of perfume, significant looks were exchanged and remarks such as 'Cor!' were exchanged. A new subject of banter and levity had been introduced.

But it was on the ground, during the night stops, that the change was really noticeable. Chaps who had previously displayed no interest whatsoever in seeing the sights or going out in the evening now positively vied with each other in suggesting to her places of interest worth a visit, or indeed, organising such outings. The conversation changed, turning away from the near inevitable 'open the hangar doors' variety, if the lady seemed bored.

It was not until the Yorks were phased out and more modern equipment appeared that stewardesses became regular members of the cabin crew. With the advent of the Hermes, the stewardesses really had arrived as permanent members of the crew. Permanent isn't the right word as they were, in fact, a very transient population, staying only a few months on average, or at most, a year or two, with some notable exceptions. Among those who didn't leave to marry, some left early in fear they would become unmarriageable. If their arrival had a devastating effect on the aircrew, they, too, could hardly fail to be affected, surrounded as they were by admiring and, often, lustful men.

Love affairs, often turbulent and hectic, became numerous.

If some of the girls were more compliant than others, this was only to be expected and led some joker to christen them 'the easy six'. The name, though unkind and probably unwarranted, stuck. I heard of one girl who, reversing roles, was determined to sleep with every member of her crew before the trip was out, and to critique their performance on the homeward journey if they felt up to it. No doubt, if she hadn't existed, she would have been invented.

At the end of the trip, on the pavement outside Hut 221, the crew members took their leave of each other and it became the scene of what were called pavement divorces. These were not the only divorces that took place, nor, I suspect, was their behaviour very different from that of any other group or profession given the same opportunity. The permissive society arrived early on the airways. It wasn't always taken very seriously and was summed up by the rather crude greeting often heard among the aircrew, 'Are you getting your share?' Nothing could illustrate better the prevailing attitude to these liaisons than the notion of a sex as a commodity to be shared out.

In the growing world of room parties, there emerged a song with the refrain, 'It's engineers' year, it's engineers' year'. At the other end of the scale, solidly based relationships and marriages did result and have stood the test of time. The aircrew themselves present a picture of apparent permanence, staying in the job for a career spanning some thirty odd years, as generation succeeds generation. The stewardesses, on the other hand, were constantly being replaced and so give the impression of a different form of permanence. As the fellows age, the girls remain perennially young, smiling and attractive.

The travelling public took the girls to their hearts and, at once, changed their name from stewardess to the more glamorous one of air hostess. In BOAC the officials dug their heels in, deleting any reference to hostesses and insisting on the name stewardess. As time went by and their numbers grew, BOAC shifted ground, naming them cabin staff (female) and eventually the unisex cabin attendant.

In the late 1960s, however, affected no doubt by the swinging sixties image of Britain, the Corporation broke out of their self-inflicted Auntie persona and horrified both passengers and staff alike by a 'Caribbean sunshine style' sales campaign, which had the girls dressed in gaily patterned paper dresses as its main feature. Leaving New York for the islands, the girls were issued with the paper garments, which had been left with the hems uncut. Given dressmakers' scissors, each girl was permitted to cut the dress to the length she herself thought suitable, and, as the mini skirt was all the rage at the time, they were mostly very short. As the cutting of hem length is not usually achieved at a first attempt, by the time the hem was even enough to pass muster, the mini was very short indeed. For such a wheeze to work at all, the dresses had to be an easy fitting, voluminous garment. One girl described it thus: 'When you bend down to serve the guy in front, he is looking right down your front, and the guy behind is looking right up your behind'.

It is somehow particularly shocking when rather severe maiden aunts suddenly abandon their blue-stocking image and emerge as swinging, 'with it' ladies. And so it was with Auntie BOAC. Fortunately, the campaign was short lived and, with the onset of the northern winter, the girls returned readily to their dark blue serge uniforms. To its credit, the Corporation was quick to realise the value of their stewardesses, and to increase their numbers. They recruited girls from their own patch; Japanese for the Tokyo route, and Indian ladies for their Indian routes, for example, to bring a knowledge of language and custom along with an additional touch of glamour to the crew.

In the Caribbean, girls from Trinidad and Jamaica were recruited. In addition to the local services from the eastern seaboard of the USA down to the islands, we operated through to the west coast of South America, arriving at Lima with the dawn and the early morning stratus. On one such trip on the VC10s, we had made it as far as Kingston and, during the transit, I took a walkabout to see how things were shaping for the departure. It didn't make much difference there when you arrived; you would be sure to be late in leaving. Something to do with the climate and the people, I think, as I never could find the reason and was invariably at a loss in completing the journey log and its ever present demand, 'State reason for delay.'

Ever hopeful that I might discover the reason, I eventually found myself back in the rear galley and there I found our charming Jamaican girl seated in the jump seat, enjoying her evening meal. Seated alongside her was a handsome lady of more mature appearance whom I'd not noticed before. Making polite conversation, I remarked that the meal looked very tempting and both ladies beamed at me with pleasure. 'I'd better introduce my mother', said the girl, 'she always brings me a snack on the way through, she knows I don't like the aircraft food'. I said 'How do you do' to her mother. 'Captain', she said, 'I'll bring you some too, if you'd like'. I thanked her politely, but refused, saying I didn't mind aircraft food; I'd got used to it by now. A thought occurred to me. I made enquiry of the mother as to how she made out with the security guards coming to and fro to the airport. 'That's no problem', she said, 'they all know me. I take my cycle, it has a basket you see, and the clean laundry and a snack. It's no trouble Captain, I can always bring another plate'.

I made my way forward again to the flight deck. The refuelling was finished so I turned off the no smoking signs. I lit a cheroot and put my feet up on the instrument panel. Outside, the tropical night was black and soft as velvet. I dismissed from my mind all thoughts of the difficult approach into Caracas or the cold Humboldt current running off Lima, steadily bringing down the cloud base to below limits. When everyone was ready and standing by, I made a leisurely start up and taxied out. Somewhere out of sight, beyond the perimeter lights, a fond mother was cycling home, the dishes from the meal cushioned by the little bundle of smalls for the laundry and thinking, perhaps, to herself, what a nice understanding man the captain was, after all.

There was one rather unpleasant trip on the Yorks. In the US experiments were being made to produce a vaccine against polio. These experiments required a supply of monkeys.

We had a regular freight run from India to the UK carrying several hundred Rhesus monkeys at a time. They were nice little creatures, if rather smelly, and the man organising the traffic was aware of this and offered extra money to the crews involved. On our behalf, the Corporation turned down the kind offer. All we got out of it was payment of the dry cleaning bill after each trip. It needed more than one session to remove the smell. Such ventilation as existed on the York was from the rear forward and the direct vision windows had to be left open for take-off. On the first such take-off out of Calcutta airport, when the full noise and fury of the four Merlin engines hit the passengers, some two hundred Rhesus monkeys evacuated their bowels together. Just as we were about to reach the rotate speed, an invisible wave of stench hit the flight deck. To eat anything at all on such a trip demanded a very strong stomach indeed and, for the Corporation to deny us a few extra shillings added insult to injury.

Unknown to me and, probably most of the crew members slogging around the routes in our converted bombers, the British government had, as far back as the dark days of 1942, set in train a sequence of events that was confidently expected to put Britain and her aircraft industry at the very forefront of the civil aircraft business when peace returned. They had formed a committee.

This committee, led by the distinguished aviator, Moore-Brabazon, had made its findings known to parliament in 1943 and aircraft designs had been formulated to match those of the USA in the Douglas DC4 and the Lockheed Constellation. The report want further and proposed a giant airliner, which was allocated to the Bristol Aeroplane Company and became the Brabazon 1. A smaller airliner with jet engines, designed to cruise at 500 mph, went to De Havilland to appear eventually as the Comet. The Bristol Britannia was another design originating from the deliberations of this committee. There were several others in BOAC which do not concern my tale.

While A V Roe were well advanced with their plans for the Tudor, Handley Page were building the Hermes, of which BOAC ordered twenty in 1948. It was the Hermes that I was destined

Jeff Gray, flying as a training captain, in the right-hand seat of a VC10.

to fly and, just as I liked the York when I first met it, I liked the Hermes. It seemed a great advance and looked the part. It had its limitations, mind you, and the chief of these involved both the engines and the airframe. The aeroplane itself was massively built and luxuriously appointed and, therefore, the greater part of the engine power was devoted to propelling this heavy structure around, leaving very little for a commercial pay load. A weight-saving exercise was set in train to try to improve its economic usefulness. More power was demanded from the engines.

Fuel was rated at 100 octane. Although something of a contradiction in terms, it is possible to make fuels with a rating of over one hundred; the scale being merely a measure of the anti-knock property, which is defined as the point when the smooth burning of the fuel ends and detonation sets in. By altering the refining process or putting more lead in the fuel, much higher values can be got. The Hermes required such a fuel. The difficulties of making this available over a great part of the world, led the Corporation to limit the Hermes routes to the African continent, this being reasonably adjacent. Indeed, the aeroplane was operated successfully over the African route network and was liked by both passengers and crew.

It was just as well to like it as 'severe disciplinary action' would be taken against anyone heard voicing a word of criticism. The old wartime edict against spreading alarm and despondency was still with us. My friend Bert, the radio officer, was overheard voicing doubts about the aeroplane and was reported to the management and given a severe wigging. From then on, Bert was loud in its praise, spoiling the effect rather at the end by adding some remark such as, 'That's what the management tells me I must say'.

The engine was of a very elegant design. It employed sleeve valves. The sleeve valve is a delightful engineering solution to the old problem of providing inlet and exhaust openings to the cylinders without the mess of push rods and cranks and external ironmongery that is more generally employed. It does, however, require a very high standard of engineering precision in manufacture and may be more generally found in motor cars where the highest standards are required and expense is unlikely to be a consideration. As you may imagine, a sleeve that slides between stationary cylinder walls and a moving piston, in addition to all this engineering precision, demands an adequate and reliable supply of lubrication lest it pick up or seize.

At this distance in time, I cannot be sure which came first; seizure to the cylinders or seizure to the pistons. The Corporation and the manufacturers made haste to introduce modifications once they found that merely haranguing the flight crews had no effect. A little thought will make it obvious why haste was needed. When a large and robust piece of machinery such as a sleeve valve seizes, becoming part of its surroundings, things come to a very abrupt stop and something has to give. What is most likely to give is the gearing connecting the propeller to the engine. They part company. The propeller in turn may part company with the aeroplane and, provided that it clears the structure and inflicts no further damage it will, with any luck, fall harmlessly away. I am not, at this stage, concerned with the safety or well-being of those below: up at the sharp end one is primarily concerned with the safety of the aeroplane and hence its occupants.

This parting of the ways, in the case of serious failure, is the brighter side of the picture. A dead windmilling propeller remaining in situ can pose a more serious hazard. Being driven by the air stream, immense drag is created and it is unlikely that the remaining engines can develop sufficient power for straight and level flight to continue. To maintain the airflow over the wings the aeroplane is forced to descend; a process that cannot be continued indefinitely and that may well be downright inconvenient.

The modifications that were introduced involved increasing the clearance between the sleeves and the pistons. I'm not sure which came first, but at each stage the lubrication was improved and a little more oil found its way past the sleeves. There was, of course, only one place for the oil to go; into the combustion chambers. The spark plugs objected. No great ill effect appeared while the engine was developing power – a little more blue smoke from the exhausts, perhaps – but trouble started when the engines were throttled back and the spark plugs were subjected to this oily mix. They began to foul up and failed to spark when required. This problem manifested itself on the descent and approach. Some thought had to be given to the operating technique to avoid periods at low power, especially if these were followed by a demand for power that might not be available. Attention then turned to the plugs and their manufacturers. All manner of modified and expensive plugs were tried but we had reached the limits of spark plug technology.

Meantime, while the operating crews did their best to avoid the problem, those staunch and marvellous fellows, the BOAC station engineers, showed what they were made of. Armed with boxes of spare plugs and spanners, they flung the cowlings open almost before the chocks were in position and the engines ceased turning. With the plugs too hot to handle, they would change every one, twenty-four plugs per engine on four engines, perched on shaky engine stands with makeshift lighting out there on the open tarmac. In addition to the normal transit checks, the aeroplane would be readied for start within the normal turn around time. That was the kind of outfit it was, and the kind of blokes they were.

Looking back, I think we did pretty well with the Hermes, not losing too many of them and operating with a fair degree of regularity and safety. We shed two propellers as I remember and only lost one aeroplane, and that was for entirely different reasons.

I tend not to see organisations as comprising individuals, but as soulless entities in their own right. Occasionally, however, this impression is corrected. The manufacturer, Handley Page, Ltd, actually comprised one very forceful individual, Sir Frederick, leading his workforce. One day, heading south for Nairobi, two charming young ladies were invited to the flight deck. 'What do you think of Daddy's aeroplane?' said one, looking at me directly. 'Marvellous', I said, 'wonderful aeroplane', taking a leaf straight from the test pilot's book. 'Good', she said, 'you know it's the engines that are the trouble'. Either the engine manufacturer lacked charming daughters or no one appeared on his behalf, so I am left with that as the final word.

***

We operated by night down through West Africa and across the Congo to Brazzaville and on to Johannesburg. This was a horrible route with a heavy accumulation of bad weather over the Cameroons and no weather radar to assist in circumventing it. By flying as high as possible in the hope of avoiding the worst of the turbulence and attendant airframe icing, you risk another ill befalling the engines; namely, carburettor icing. To combat this means selecting a supply of hot air to the engines, which at once decreases their power output and, flying near the performance ceiling, enforces a descent into the murk below. The high ground precluded tackling the route at lower altitude. We proceeded as best we could, coping with the problems as circumstances dictated and keeping a calm sough, as the Scots say.

Here I noticed a very strange thing in some of the captains. Where one might have thought that, with their aeroplanes beset with dangers, they would have been glued to their seats, some would leave the flight deck and drift off back to the lights and warmth of the galley or passenger cabin, leaving their co-pilot and crew to struggle on without them. I had also noticed that occasionally, in 'giving away' landings to their co-pilot, they gave away some of the trickier ones, sometimes adopting the role of instructor or mentor; a role for which they clearly had neither talent nor training. And so, in learning my business, I learnt not just from the better captains but from the less able as well, and resolved, in my secret book of golden rules, that I would not be one of those. When things get tough, the captain's place is at the controls. I was already beginning to conclude that the days when the captain strolled among his passengers, bestowing a word here and stopping for a chat there, were over, indeed I doubted if they had ever arrived. Since I was not of a particularly sociable disposition and the role didn't suit me anyway, this was a convenient conclusion to arrive at.

A promotion to command, although at times appearing far off, was ever present in my mind and I tried always to believe that, were it to come on the very next flight, I should be ready for it. Meantime, as I slogged around the routes, great events marking the progress of civil aviation in which I had no part came and went. Rather, just as I had missed the invasion of Europe during the war, I missed the Berlin airlift and also the airlift that accompanied the partition of India into the new and uneasy states of Pakistan and India. Far away, in another continent, that of South America, British South American Airways (BSAA) were conducting their affairs in such a way as to affect my chances of promotion, however unlikely and trivial this must seem in the overall scheme of things.

I still think of them as the Pathfinders of earlier wartime days, if only because their chief was the old pathfinder leader and the pilots I knew there were mostly ex-pathfinder bomber pilots. They had a thing about stars. Their aircraft were dubbed star liners and stewardesses were star girls. But it was an ill-fated star. Every airline appeared to have a share of misfortune, of aircraft incidents and accidents. Nor did this always appear to be related to how well or ill they conducted their affairs. The aeroplanes of that time were subject to all the rigours and hazards of the elements in which they flew and the standard of equipment, both on board and on the ground, often fell woefully short of the task demanded of them. In such circumstances, it was to be expected that human failures would combine and lead to disaster. BSAA seemed to have more than their fair share, and then came the Tudors.

While BOAC battled mightily not to have the Tudors, having set their hearts on American equipment, BSAA was convinced that the Tudor exactly fitted their requirements. Although it came from a different manufacturer than the Hermes, the Tudor was from the same stable. I have no first-hand knowledge of the machine, nor have I ever met anyone able to explain what defects beset them and so, to me, their terrible habit of disappearing without trace in mid-flight remains shrouded in mystery. There has to be some explanation: nonsense about Bermuda triangles will not do. The British government intervened to vanish BSAA and amalgamate them with BOAC. The Corporation then won some further routes in which they had little interest and some aeroplanes for which they had no use, together with additional staff, particularly pilots, who were not, I regret to say, welcomed with open arms by their compatriots, myself included.

There was little to be done about it. Guarantees of equitable treatment had been given them and they were to be slotted into the existing pilot force as if they had gained their positions and seniority with BOAC. No comparable safeguards were forthcoming for those of us in BOAC who were, perforce, displaced downwards. It was rumoured and widely believed that they had glimpsed the chopper coming and hastily promoted co-pilots to junior captain rank and junior captains to senior captain rank. All that could be rescued was the arrangement whereby the newcomers were to be frozen in their enhanced positions until the rules governing promotion in BOAC caught up with them. Even at this distance in time, it is difficult not to be prejudiced by this turn of events and to separate fact from fiction. I do not really believe that they were capable of such a trick, merely that in BSAA, promotion had been more rapid. I still hold to the view, however, that such a thing should never have happened. They should have been recruited, if needed, starting at the bottom where everyone else had to start. Life, however, is not always fair, and the rules enshrined in the Boys' Own Paper, are not always applied.

On the Hermes, messenger to the gods, command prospects were becoming brighter. Promotion from the right-hand seat was not yet company-wide policy. If vacancies arose on your fleet you were in line for promotion. The days of retraining others to keep in step from a different fleet had not yet arrived. Acting, as it turned out, on their own initiative, the fleet began a programme of command training. I devoured it, passing the final check-out flight with the fleet captain without hesitation. And then the blow fell: the fleet was to be disbanded and the aeroplanes sold off if a buyer could be found.

By this time a new sound was heard in the skies. The first of a new generation of aircraft had appeared: the Comets. In their day and time they created the same sort of interest and excitement that was not to recur until the advent of Concorde. The banshee howl of the jet engine, now so familiar, had entered the civilian aircraft business and, incidentally, created a whole new protest industry campaigning against aircraft noise. This was to play a great part in our lives.

I had refrained from volunteering to join the Comet fleet. As is always the case with new equipment, the crews were being specially selected. I had no doubt that I, too, could be specially selected, but there was more chance of promotion by staying where I was, and I stayed put. And when the new has become accepted and familiar, then anyone can be specially selected.

When the Hermes packed up, I felt that I had, perhaps, some claim for special consideration, and said so to the fleet captain. He promised to do whatever he could, unless of course I had some impossible demand in mind, such as going on the Atlantic route. That's what I had in mind: the impossible dream and as a co-pilot of course.

He was a rare breed of manager and as good as his word. A small group of us were posted to Filton in Bristol to start a conversion course to the Stratocruiser. It could not have come at a worse time from my personal and family viewpoint. My wife was pregnant, the child was expected when I would be away in Bristol, and the plans I had made to be at home, not just for the event, but to look after my two small sons had to be abandoned. My wife and I discussed the problem and came to quite the wrong conclusions. We decided I should go on the course and we could try to get someone, probably my sister or my mother, to come and keep house. It was not to be. Try as we might, we were forced back on the expedient of putting the boys into a residential nursery while my wife went into hospital. It was disastrous and they hated it. Nearly as much as we hated doing it to them. When my wife came home with the new baby, having had a bad time, and I collected the boys, we were a sorry and unhappy family. It nearly broke my heart. It still does.

The author (centre) with the crew of an Avro York.

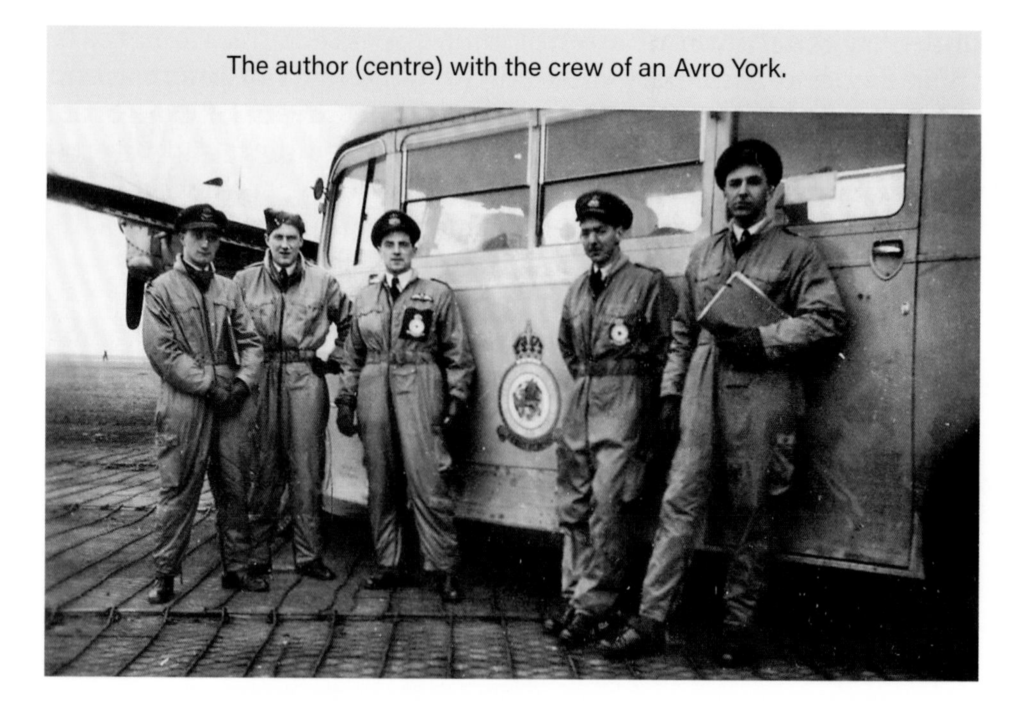

The hired hands

The Boeing Stratocruiser was the queen of the skies over the Atlantic. It was advertised and hailed as the epitome of luxury in air travel and, indeed, looking back, it has never been seriously rivalled. There was a pleasant and intimate horseshoe bar in the lower lobe for travellers to refresh themselves before having a sumptuous dinner, and sleeping bunks were available to cross the wastes of the Atlantic in the best possible position; the horizontal.

In what would otherwise have been the sharp end, but was in fact blunt and bulbous, the flight deck was a commodious affair like a greenhouse, housing a full complement of captain and crew. There were two pilots, later to become three when the flight-time regulations came into force, two flight engineers to cater for the complexities of the four Pratt and Whitney power units, each driving a massive Hamilton Standard four-bladed hollow propeller, a specialist navigator and a radio officer. The very best of the Company's chief stewards and stewardesses catered for the passengers, themselves very often people of importance and influence shuttling on business or pleasure between the old world and the new.

The truth of the matter, however, was that the aeroplane lacked the range necessary to make the west-bound crossing against the prevailing winds and, only on very rare occasions with unusual weather patterns, could the crossing be made direct without recourse to a refuelling stop. So it became a matter of careful planning and tactics; each flight being unique and having to be tackled rather in the manner of a man swinging from a trapeze. This was the graphic description supplied to me by the chief training captain. 'Don't let go of one bar', he cautioned, 'until the next is within your grasp lest you should fall in the middle without the benefit of any kind of safety net'. The great circle track, the shortest distance between two points between London and New York, passes close to Gander in Newfoundland. There at Gander, built for the wartime North Atlantic aircraft ferry, lay the keystone of the operation.

The first leg was to get from London to Gander against the headwinds with sufficient reserves of fuel to cater for navigational contingencies en route and the likelihood of adverse weather in the maritime states on arrival. That done, the flight down the eastern seaboard to New York was fairly routine. Were that not possible at the planning stage, one further step remained, to fly to Shannon in Ireland to refuel and thus shorten the distance, albeit only slightly. Some further juggling with the figures might then be possible, using a high degree of judgement and weather lore, to accept a reduction in reserves and the closest possible alternate airfield to Gander. Now we get to the trapeze analogy. When the flight lumbered off from Shannon, climbing slowly along the estuary to bid farewell to land at the Kilkee marker, its destination at this stage was the critical point on the crossing where it was just as quick to continue to Gander as to return to Shannon. The next destination was the point of no return. By then a firm decision, whether to proceed or not, had to be made. Meanwhile, it was hoped that the radio officer had gleaned sufficient information of the revised weather forecasts for the maritime states and, more importantly, recorded all or some of the actual reports, and the navigator had the position and times at each 10 degrees of longitude plotted, and an exact knowledge of the all-important wind component experienced so far. The fuel used, and that remaining, completed the picture upon which a decision had to be made. Here it was that a knowledge of the route and its weather patterns, coupled with the ability and confidence to make decisions, came together. All of this I now had to learn.

When winds or weather precluded such a flight, there was

one further major alternative route, via Keflavik in Iceland and thence across Greenland to Goose Bay in Labrador and so to New York. Up there, near the Arctic Circle there were other difficulties to be assessed and dealt with. There was no alternative airfield to Keflavik and the weather there is notoriously fickle. To be prudent, the flight had to carry sufficient fuel to return to Prestwick in Scotland should this become necessary, with Keflavik out in adverse weather. The aircraft could carry such a large reserve of fuel only at the cost of landing overweight on arrival which was not permitted. So the reserve fuel had to be restricted to a point about an hour's flight time short of Keflavik and a decision made at or before that point as to go on or not. Once committed, the flight droned on to Iceland, From there, bearing away towards Greenland's icy mountains, Goose Bay was well within range, with Gander and the other maritime airports as alternatives and, apart from the navigational and communication difficulties inherent in the route, another safe crossing could be achieved.

In all this there were many compensating advantages and rewards. The long winter nights brought forth the northern lights in glorious display. 'Or like the borealis race, That flit ere you can point their place', said Burns. In the summer, flying in the eerie twilight, with the sun barely below the northern horizon, I thought of another Scotsman, David Livingstone: 'scenes so lovely must have been gazed upon by angels in their flight'. Dominie Grant may have been pleased to know that his efforts to instil some knowledge of such people could sharpen my appreciation.

The satisfaction of contending with the elements and taking part in deploying the skills and knowledge necessary so to do, brought its own rewards. There was a lot of adverse weather to contend with. The aeroplane is sensitive to icing and, although sufficiently equipped with anti-icing gear, it had its limitations. Nightly there were Atlantic depressions and fronts to be crossed. If the aeroplane was allowed to accumulate ice in any quantity, its performance was reduced and the airspeed began to decay rapidly. A lower and warmer layer had to be sought before the equipment became overtaxed and the engines, although set at maximum power and guzzling precious fuel, were defeated by the falling airspeed. After instructing the radio officer to advise air traffic control of departure from the assigned level and, if necessary to declare *force majeure*, the autopilot had to be disengaged and height traded for speed until either a warmer level was found or the conditions were left behind in the onward flight. The whirling Hamilton Standard propellers would signal our departure from icing conditions by shedding their ice in chunks, which struck against the ice plates on the fuselage. If the captain had chosen this time to take to the bunk and rest a while during the crossing, nothing could be guaranteed to bring him back to the flight deck so quickly as the sound of ice upon ice plates.

In this different world of the North Atlantic that I had entered, there were other differences too. The captains were mostly the most senior and experienced of the Company's pilots, having gravitated there as of right and not merely because of the extra pay and allowances that the route attracted, though no doubt, these were a factor. They were known as the Atlantic barons. No description I can think of could be more apt. They behaved much as I imagine the barons of old had done, secure in their position and authority and demanding allegiance to themselves. The range of human eccentricity and individuality is very wide and, regretfully, the job was beginning to demand a uniformity of operational procedures and thought that was alien to them. It is tempting to tell of the legends that grew up about them, but I must resist lest they be misunderstood, and content myself with recording that I learnt a great deal from them. Not all of it could be applied either by reason of my own shortcomings or of the changes at work in our affairs, but at least I was privileged to have known what real aircraft commanders were like in the heyday of the breed.

The co-pilots had to cultivate their own skills and attributes. It was unusual, and indeed rare, for them to be given take-offs or landings to do, and we tended to worry about this in case the lack of practice eroded our judgement and skills. We were expected to play our part in looking after the ship during the long and often tedious crossing, while the captain saved himself for the difficult decisions and the landings. We had to acquire and maintain the highest possible standard of instrument flying and procedural work to bring the aeroplane down to the limits set for landing, so that when the approach or runway lights appeared through the murk, all the dials were behaving, the aeroplane was tracking the centre line, the speed and rate of descent were right on the button and everything was set for the landing.

One further accomplishment was required. The spread of the airways and their attendant reporting points, coupled with the immense growth of traffic in North America was putting stress upon the air traffic control system. The authorities were slow in developing and deploying equipment to keep abreast of these changes. It had become necessary, to avoid error and to separate the traffic, for every air traffic clearance to detail each and every airway and reporting point en route, along with each and every flight level, and pass this clearance to the aircraft over the air for the co-pilot to record and read back. Air traffic control frequencies became increasingly congested. During busy periods the controller had to recourse to giving the clearances in the gaps, stringing together without pause clearances for several aircraft waiting in line. Each aeroplane, then, in turn, choosing his time, read back his clearance. Read it back word for word, without altering the sequence or omitting anything so that the controller could more easily cross check it. This otherwise simple and relatively undemanding task was raised almost to an art form and demanded immense concentration and an encyclopaedic knowledge of the airways and air traffic control procedures. Every co-pilot strove to attain the highest standard of professionalism, as every call and reply had an audience of waiting and listening critics, each ready with a caustic witticism to greet any goof.

It was helpful also to develop a rhythm and manner of speech which the North American ear could identify and understand. To read straight back in a plummy English accent was guaranteed to throw the controller right out and necessitate no end of 'say again' and repetition. We developed for this, what was called a mid-Atlantic accent that attracted derision from our colleagues in the UK and in Europe, where they had no need or understanding of this strategy. The straight navigators played a huge and vital part in the North Atlantic operation. Their main navigational aid was a radio broadcasting system known as Loran (long-range navigation). It required skilful interpretation in obtaining position lines, and hence fixes, particularly at dawn and dusk, and when sunspot activity played a hand in distorting the signals.

I have already been at pains to try to explain that navigation is nothing without aids to enable the navigator to fix his position. It was here where the air marshalls failed, in the period between the wars, to equip their bomber forces to find their way, or science failed to devise such systems, that led to the early failures of the bomber offensive.

The chain of Loran stations covering most of the Atlantic, made navigation possible. Radio signals travel further at night than by day, and this forced the night crossing upon us and made daytime crossings difficult. In consequence, we were operating into the Maritime airports in the early morning and dawn periods when the fogs and poor visibility, which afflict Newfoundland with its Labrador current, are at their worst.

The navigators became very skilled in their interpretation of Atlantic weather systems and acquired an unsurpassed knowledge of the winds aloft and of the jet streams that exist there. This knowledge and experience was invaluable to the captains and, when at length my turn came, I was content to draw heavily upon it.

Technology in the shape of radio telephony or speech transmission was replacing communication by Morse code and bringing close the demise of the specialist radio officer. The Corporation was anxious for pilots to take over these duties and it must have appeared to the radio officers that the pilots, egged on by the prospect of extra remuneration, were just as anxious to do so. Not unnaturally, this gave rise to ill feeling based upon anxiety for the future and both the navigators and the flight engineers expressed their sympathy for the plight of the radio officers, tempered no doubt, with the feeling that their turn might come. The Corporation went out of its way to help them, offering courses in flying training or specialist navigation for those who wanted them or seemed likely to benefit from them, and what was at the time considered fairly generous severance terms for the others. It was one of the many subjects of heated debate in the hostelries and other establishments along Third Avenue favoured by the crews as meeting places.

New York was a bonus. I felt that Samuel Johnson might be brought up to date. 'When a man is tired of New York, he is tired of life'. Following a crossing it was thought necessary to have a local night in bed. This meant two whole days in New York per trip. There were things to do and to see in abundance.

When the Number Three line base, for reasons of economy and to save precious hard currency for Britain, was brought back to Bristol from Montreal, the Corporation and Bristol City put their heads together to make the move from the plush apartments and allowances of North America a little more palatable. High standard executive housing was provided in Bristol for the staff at modest, if unsubsidised, rentals. They retained their extra pay and allowances. Newcomers to the fleet, such as myself, did not, however, benefit. Where we did score, along with the others, was that a subsistence allowance, paid in dollars, was made in lieu of board on the Atlantic routes.

Things were thought expensive in New York at that time and the allowances for food were generous. The crew members were adept at finding inexpensive eating places where nourishing meals could be had in pleasant surroundings, saving their dollars to purchase other things or to put away in a savings account, incurring the risk of displeasure from HM Inland Revenue or exchange control.

Of particular interest to me was the thriving do-it-yourself trade. This phenomenon of modern life had arrived much earlier in North America than elsewhere and shops and warehouses abounded, selling tools and materials for the home handyman. Here, much earlier than in Europe, the realisation that high wages made the servicing and repair of ordinary domestic appliances and equipment prohibitively expensive, led people to tackle these repairs themselves and, once they realised how simple it all was, a thriving trade was born, which later crossed the Atlantic. The transatlantic trade was not all one way. The high fidelity boom, as yet unnamed, originated in Britain when the Decca record company made their first micro groove records and amateur radio enthusiasts turned their attention to designing and making amplifiers and associated equipment to match this new standard of sound reproduction. This quickly spread to North America, and New York at the time was full of places dedicated to such enthusiasts, where the components were cheaper and do-it-yourself kits and test equipment were more readily available. In time the large commercial radio firms became interested and Britain soon lost her early lead to America.

The Stratocruiser fleet also served Bermuda and the Caribbean from the North American side and there were regular services across the Atlantic to Montreal. In the bitter winter weather there, one enterprising travel agent posted up the water temperatures in Bermuda and Nassau in his shop window. I hope it brought him business as I thought that he deserved it. In late summer the Caribbean is prone to hurricanes. These revolving tropical storms form over the warm waters of the Gulf and develop a circulation and life of their own. They bring the threat of damage and destruction to the islands within their path and to the mainland coastal areas of the USA. Obeying the forces generated by the earth's rotation, these storms take a curved path turning to the right, eventually heading out into the Atlantic. Occasionally, this puts Bermuda within their path. Revolving tropical storms are known in several parts of the world and the name changes with the different regions, being variously described as typhoons, hurricanes or cyclones, with a variety of local names thrown in. In Bermuda and the Caribbean they are called hurricanes.

We arrived in Bermuda from Trinidad with a hurricane hard on our heels. The aeroplane went on its way to New York as we arrived at the Princess Hotel at Hamilton. The captain went on his separate way to the Mid Ocean Club. Behind us another crew arrived and, whether because it was scheduled to do so, or for some other reason, their aeroplane was left at the airport.

In the path of an oncoming hurricane, aeroplanes that cannot be flown out have to be secured and tethered to the ground lest they be blown over or damaged by the storm. As the wind increased in velocity and Bermuda battened itself down, the atmosphere in the hotel became hectic. People rushed about excitedly in nervous anticipation, drinking too much or otherwise displaying their fears and anxiety.

Out on the field at Kinley someone noticed the unattended Stratocruiser and became anxious for its safety. The crew who had left it there, headed by one of the most senior and therefore most feared of the Atlantic barons, were called upon to do something. At this late stage little could be done except to get the crew out to the airfield to start up the engines and head the aeroplane into the wind and so ride out the storm. While they thus occupied themselves we joined in the party spirit in the hotel. Outside the fury of the wind grew, the hotel building shook and rattled and within, the excited guests proceeded to eat, drink and be merry.

At some ungodly hour, the telephone rang. It was the call to arms. Out on the field relief was needed. We boarded the coach and drove slowly and carefully through the fallen and flying debris to the airfield. We took over from the night watchmen who explained that they had to leave to get some sleep to be ready for their next assignment. This made very little sense to me, but my captain, a fairly junior chap, made no demur. The aeroplane was nicely located on an open piece of tarmac, headed into the wind and facing a boundary fence. Caught up in the fence were pieces of paper and cloth and, here and there, sheets of corrugated iron arrested in their flight. Flying objects, particularly sheets of corrugated iron, are one of the hazards of hurricanes. These tattered objects made excellent wind indicators caught in the glare of the landing lights and the captain fell to concentrating on the business in hand and steering into the wind. Left with little to do, I looked about me and chatted with the control tower officer about the conditions. Surprisingly, his equipment was still functioning and the wind speed gauges still reading. They are often an early casualty. It seemed to me to be moderating. When I got around to the fuel gauges and realised that we were running low, it became clear why the previous crew were so anxious to be off, quite apart from anything they had told us. Very shortly now we would run out of fuel and the engines would stop. I pointed this out to the captain who said nothing and sat there in a fever of indecision. I didn't like it any more than he did but it was evident that we would have to refuel. It was unlikely that the refuellers would want to do that, given the conditions. There were no securing points available on the field, that we could move to and tie the thing down.

'Sandbags', I said, 'we need to get some chocks in with sandbags to hold them, then we can shut down and refuel'. There was some argument about this. When I called for a better idea, none was forthcoming. We proceeded with the plan. I felt quite confident that once we had sufficient fuel on board we could safely leave the aeroplane. A heavily loaded Stratocruiser could only be persuaded to leave the ground by dint of running all the engines at high power for a considerable length of time and achieving a speed far in excess of anything the retreating hurricane could produce. It is easy to be confident when you don't have to carry the can.

When the refuelling was completed we started up again. The dawn came and the storm seemed less fearsome, although the debris lay about and the sea was raging. I ventured another suggestion. 'The wind', I said, 'is backing towards the runway direction. If we got the passengers out here we could get off in a couple of hours'. If we didn't get moving, by the time our opposite numbers came to the airport the wind would be across the runway again and outside limits, and they'd be further delayed. This plan would have the additional benefit of getting us home a couple of days early and the other crew would be late, having to pick up our trip. I thought I'd made a cast-iron case. We went on running the engines. Presently I could hear the Pan Am Clipper from New York for Bermuda calling Kinley approach for his descent. I put it up on the loud speaker. He seemed unconcerned by the weather report.

After a while we could see a Stratocruiser on finals, rocking about a good deal. He touched down and taxied in. He kept all the equipment clear, stopping in front of the terminal and disembarked the passengers through the cargo bays and down the built-in steps. When he was happy, he shut down the motors, had the fuel topped up, boarded the joining passengers in the same way and made his departure.

After a bit we shut down the engines and went back to the hotel. The hurricane continued its retreat into the Atlantic, filling gradually. The wind changed behind it as it was bound to do, getting across the runway and effectively closing the field for the rest of the day. We checked out that night as passengers on a DC6 for New York to continue our trip as planned. On the way, I confessed to the navigator that I never could remember which was which between veering and backing when dealing with surface winds. He remembered and told me. I've forgotten again.

In New York we had, perforce, to spend some time on stand-by duties. In general we covered the service one hour ahead of our own. It was a fairly comfortable arrangement and eminently sensible. When weather or mechanical failures disrupted the schedules, some reshuffling of crews became necessary. One morning in January, we were called out to take a relief flight from New York to Goose Bay, Labrador. One of our aeroplanes was broken down there. The weather in Goose was poor but we could muster two alternative fields and the rules permitted us to go. We got airborne from Idlewild and, hardly had we settled in the climb when the captain's window cracked with an almighty bang. We re-cleared back to Idlewild. Pan Am had a spare and were willing to part with it. By the time repairs had been effected the day was far advanced but the weather at

Goose had steadily improved and the relief flight set out again.

In Goose Bay we found a forlorn-looking Stratocruiser parked on the snow-covered tarmac, but the passengers were a cheerful crowd and obviously glad to see us. I noticed that the flaps on the parked Stratocruiser had been left in the extended position and looked as if they had been damaged. I sought out my counterpart, the first officer. He was very glum. There is a particular kind of glumness that afflicts men involved in aircraft accidents; a combination of guilt, bitter regret and self-condemnation. 'What happened?' I asked. 'We were low on the approach', he said; 'at least, I thought we were low. I warned the captain. Mind you, it was all white but the runway didn't look right. We hit a snow bank out on the approach – you can see the wheel marks – and bounced off it. It's rock hard, but we made it to the runway. We landed all right but the flaps are holed and damaged'. He bitterly condemned himself for not taking over. 'If only, if only' was his refrain. I asked what the 'old man' had to say about it. He told me that this was what worried him most of all: he didn't seem to know what he'd done. 'I don't think he believes it. He doesn't believe he hit the snow bank. I took him out there to show him the wheel marks'.

We boarded the passengers and cranked up for London. They'd had a great time and were delighted to be on their way again. Bob Boothby[1] was one of the passengers. He came on the flight deck and chatted. 'We were very lucky', he claimed, 'if we hadn't had such a marvellous pilot, we could all have been killed'.

Time and advancing years began to take their toll among the North Atlantic barons and, slowly, like the legendary old soldiers they were, they began to fade away. 'Not before time', was the verdict. But that must be the verdict on each and every passing generation by its successors. They were unique in that they were the first to complete a career in aviation and so it was a real job, after all, and it was possible to stay the course and, perhaps one day, insurance companies would recognise this

1 Robert Lord (Bob) Boothby (1900–1986) was a Conservative politician, author and broadcaster.

and stop demanding extra premiums, or even governments, and we should gain recognition and special arrangements for voting overseas, just like the merchant marine.

Aviators were more readily accepted and without comment in North America. The job there was already held to be quite ordinary and, together with this acceptance, it attracted good pay. The British lagged far behind. Indeed, the driver of the Carey coach who drove us from the airfield to the city was better paid than most senior BOAC captains.

One evening in New York, and quite by chance, my friend Jack and I met one of the Pan American captains. Pan American and BOAC were rivals in the North Atlantic but, in reality cooperated closely. If an aeroplane went sick and a flight had to be abandoned the commercial load was at once offered to the rival line. There was a strong spirit of friendly competition between the two. Between the Pan American pilots and those of BOAC a great gulf between their pay and reward set them poles apart. Our new-found friend was in town as a member of the American Airline Pilots' Association, (ALPA) engaged in squeezing more pay out of the Pan American vice-presidents, as he put it.

For whatever reason, he decided to lay it on the line for Jack and me. The day will never dawn, he predicted, when your vice-presidents will see their way clear to paying you more. 'In aviation', he said, 'we are the hired hands. Nothing more or less. Just so long as you hold down your licence, you stay hired. In Pan Am', he said, 'I want to see the line captains the highest paid men in the company, next only to the company president'. 'What of the vice-presidents', I cried, 'and the management captains; behind them, surely?' 'Hell no', was the reply, 'you don't have to worry about those guys, they'll always be there, ten a penny and you may rely on them to look out for themselves'. The plain truth of what he said struck home and his expression, 'hired hands', stuck in my mind. From time to time since then, I took note that my acquaintance continued to exert great influence on ALPA affairs, so clearly his principles had stood the test of time, to the great benefit of the hired hands.

Like the Hermes, the Stratocruiser suffered from problems of seized engines and shedding propellers. The other major operator, Pan American, shared these problems and we drew comfort from that and the knowledge that the US aviation authorities took more than a passive interest in matters affecting flight safety. About the time I joined the fleet they had in fact been grounded for a spell while the problems of engine seizure were investigated. The oil dilution system came under suspicion. This was a device whereby, under extremely cold conditions, the engine oil could be diluted with neat fuel, making starting easier. Over-free usage had brought on the problem, as the engines were being subjected to a lack of lubrication, during and after start up.

There are a number of imponderables in the career of an airline pilot. There is the manifest risk of being involved in an incident or, worse still, an aircraft accident. In the event of surviving such a disaster, it is almost certain that where blame has to be apportioned the pilot or pilots will receive a due allotment. Pilot error is the most prevalent finding in accident investigation. There also is the risk of losing your licence on medical grounds or failing to qualify in one of the periodic tests or examinations.

In times past in BOAC there were several other ways by which your career could come to a sudden halt. Chief among the Corporation's fears was that we might talk to the press. We were bound to silence by our contract and periodically warning notices were circulated restating the dire penalties for non-compliance. It was rather like the Official Secrets Act that today binds all government officials and servants of the crown to utter and absolute silence.

We shared this silly notion with the Corporation. If only we were free to reveal all to the public, 'they' wouldn't dare to do this or that, and what power we would wield over them. Just what these secrets were that carried with them such clout or made their revelation such a crime was never clear to me. The press continued to display very little interest in our affairs other than when an aeroplane got bent or the Corporation had piled up more losses for the taxpayer to support. As for the technical press, the British were blessed with two excellent publications that I read when they came my way to increase my knowledge of aviation affairs and those of the Corporation in particular.

Communication with the press was known to be the one sure way of being fired. Whereas the Services have recourse to a blanket condemnation, 'Conduct prejudicial to good order and discipline', covering a multitude of sins, the Corporation was less favourably placed. In their list of what constituted misbehaviour likely to incur 'severe disciplinary action', the wording, 'not in front of the passengers' featured prominently. Among these crimes, drinking, that is, drinking in uniform, in public places, or less than eight hours before flight, was rightly taboo. Occasionally, but without real conviction, 'no smoking in public', or perhaps less severely, 'refrain from smoking in front of the public,' was added. Many things constituted misbehaviour. Over the course of the years, I knew several chaps who became alcoholics. They continued to drink until they had all but destroyed themselves and, usually, they were pulled up by the training section, who were the first to notice the deterioration in their performance. But perhaps they didn't do it in front of the public for, if they had, they would certainly have been reported much earlier.

I don't like to think about it but I was once accused of drinking before going on duty. There was no justification whatsoever in the charge, but that made it all the more frightening, not less. Bermuda was one of the slip stations where it was easy to get into trouble. On an island given over to tourists, most of whom arrive and depart by air, it is difficult not to be seen by the public. Having a gin and tonic at lunch time in a bar along Front Street was almost bound to attract notice. The BOAC station manager had his office on Front Street. He had the reputation of being anti-aircrew and being ever eager to report cases of misbehaviour, real or imaginary, back to London. On this occasion, I had gone into Hamilton with some of my crew.

The captain wasn't there, of course. He stayed in another hotel away from his crew. The senior flight engineer wasn't there either; he was indulging in a passionate love affair with a stewardess and was lost to us, having joined the cabin crew. We stopped for refreshment in a British-style pub on Front Street and, hardly had we entered when we were recognised by a group of young Americans as their crew. They were staying, as it turned out, in the same hotel.

After a few pleasantries, and a drink with them, we had to decline their invitation to a 'wingding' party that night as we were due out at midnight with a call around nine-thirty. We had to take a rain check. Pickup that night was around ten-thirty P M. As luck would have it, the third pilot and I came down together and, in making our way to the foyer, passed the room where the wingding was in progress. It was just breaking up but had obviously been hugely successful. We were dragged in to say hi to the party and to be shown off by our new friends. Someone suggested they all come to see us off, so amidst scenes of merriment and much hubbub, we were escorted to the front desk and out to the transport. There were two transports and the cabin crew had already boarded one along with the chief flight engineer. They were ready to move off and, seeing a mob descending on them, they did so without further ado. We got away when the company had wished us Godspeed and happy landings and the girls had kissed everyone soundly. At the airport, the captain was hovering nervously on the pavement by the bus stop. He took me aside as soon as I stepped from the coach. He looked put out. He tried to explain to me that the cabin staff were refusing to fly on the basis that the technical crew had been drinking. The chief flight engineer had been appointed spokesman. The captain looked more and more uncomfortable as he spoke, as it seemed such patent nonsense. It gradually dawned on me that this was no laughing matter. They weren't talking of a couple of beers at lunchtime, well outside the eight-hour rule, but of a drinking session extending throughout the afternoon and evening.

This malicious accusation had to be squarely faced. 'Best get the station manager out here', I said, 'and a company doctor while we're about it, Let's get this lie nailed down straight away'. The captain began to fuss and worry about the service being delayed. 'It's too late to think of that, matey', I thought to myself. 'I'm not the one refusing to fly'. Eventually I settled for an apology from the cabin staff and an additional one from that son of a bitch flight engineer. Just what his part in all this was completely eluded me. Perhaps some imaginary slight by me, some unspoken criticism of his behaviour, had upset him or his beloved and they had seized upon what looked like an opportunity for mischief-making.

I had one other close call for misbehaviour stakes, in Bermuda. There were complaints one morning from the hotel management about a noisy BOAC crew party. There were two crews there overnight. The hotel manager was sufficiently incensed to complain directly to BOAC. Our man on the spot had contacted the two captains, who were minding their own business at the other end of the island. The most senior of the two came over directly to hold an inquiry; a summary of evidence. When I was interviewed I knew nothing of it. I knew there had been a noisy party and in which room, but noisy room parties in that particular tourist hotel were a nightly occurrence and unlikely to occasion comment unless they happened to be next door. I thought the facts spoke for themselves. The room where the party allegedly took place was that of my opposite number on the other crew. Moreover, he had appeared at breakfast sporting a black eye that he claimed was from walking into the bathroom door; a variation of the old chestnut about contracting things from sitting on toilet seats. I felt that even the most senior of captains wouldn't have too much trouble arriving at a decision and, indeed, I was quite right. A few days later, when I was in New York, I received a polite note from him thanking me for assisting him with his enquiries and effectively exonerating me from any part in the affair. Naturally, I felt that was that, and put the matter from my mind. Some weeks later, much to my astonishment, I was summoned to the fleet manager's office.

I found another crewman there, waiting in the outer office. I asked him if he knew what this was about. 'Everyone who was there is to get a reprimand', he told me. 'They weren't pleased with what old Charlie did, just getting that lot to apologise. They're getting loss of seniority as well, so we're lucky'. My friend was fearful that I would raise objections, and pleaded with me not to start anything. He need not have worried. I am ashamed to say that I accepted the reprimand as meekly as he had done, insisting only that the letter from my senior captain friend be placed alongside it in the record. You occasionally have to accept no-win situations.

Eventually the long-awaited command course was upon me. When promotion is rapid and, hence commonplace, no great emphasis is laid upon command courses, but where it is long delayed and infrequent, command courses are elevated in importance. The command course itself, designed originally to assist candidates and ensure that they are prepared and fit for the task, becomes an immense hurdle to be overcome. It bars the way to promotion for which the candidate should already be prepared. At this stage the course itself, while assuming increased importance had not yet become a major barrier. It was basically designed to give a revision in handling, to make good the neglect of years in the right-hand seat, pounding the circuit at Shannon with a training captain alongside. The real test lay in the series of flights that followed, on the route, in command and under supervision.

The first such flight, scheduled for the 20 December 1957, sticks in my mind. I reported at Hut 221 on the north side of Heathrow airport in the usual way. The supervisory captain failed to appear at the appointed time, so I proceeded to the briefing room without him. Some minor hitch had no doubt delayed him. At the briefing, the flight planner's analysis of the North Atlantic weather charts showed that we had a very marginal operation indeed. If it was to go at all, it meant a refuelling stop at Shannon, then to Gander with a minimum reserve. There was no operation possible through Keflavik, the weather there and at Prestwick being way below limits. The Shannon weather was also marginal, forecast to be below limits for a major part of the time. It was just the sort of nasty start I could have done without. It was a toss up whether to scrub altogether or venture as far as Shannon in the hope of finding conditions there which were within, or better than, limits, with fuel to return, using London as alternative.

Just ahead of me, the captain taking the other Stratocruiser service of the night, had already cancelled. His service however, was due to operate through Prestwick and this gave him an additional problem that led him to scrub without hesitation. As you move away from the centre of things and take one step back, you enter another realm. I was aware that the news that one service had scrubbed and the other was going, would cross the apron carried on the grapevine, apparently without the benefit of human agency. I was further aware that it would be known that the experienced captain had scrubbed and some sprog first officer under supervision had elected to go. That there might be different reasons or circumstances for doing so would not arise in these debates. I decided to go and gave the instructions to set things in train.

The supervisory captain arrived shortly afterwards. Without saying anything he would know that I would have gone ahead without him up to the decision stage, but without as yet alerting the stand-by. I could see that he was puzzled by the fact that I had gone ahead and decided on a course of action. A horrible suspicion dawned upon me. It just wasn't possible that he didn't know that I was under supervision, not possible that something so important to me meant so little to anyone else and he had not been advised. Not possible, I knew, that the training file, so meticulously put together, had not been studied but lay, along with the blank supervisory forms gathering dust, forgotten and neglected on some desk within the Kremlin.[2] But it *was* possible. That was the kind of outfit it was and the kind of people they were.

He took it fairly well. As we left the building and walked

2 Nickname for BOAC's headquarters

across the rain-swept tarmac, dodging the dimly lit vehicles that careered about among the parked aeroplanes I could sense his worries clicking away. 'Don't worry', I said, 'we're not going to bend anything, not even the rules'. I became aware that the activity among the vehicles was centred on my aeroplane. I collared the first two-ringer I saw and demanded to know what the hell was going on. The loading should have been finished long ago, where was this stuff coming from? Of course, I might have guessed. They were taking whatever load they could from the cancelled flight and stuffing it on to mine, regardless of the fact that every extra kilogram reduced my chances of an operation out of Shannon. They had, in fact, already killed it completely. I put on my best imitation of a North Atlantic baron. 'Get that stuff out of here, get that stuff off my aeroplane', I said. Nothing happened. The two-ringer came back. 'There'll be a delay', he said, 'getting that stuff off will cause a delay'. Causing a delay was the ultimate crime. Just in case that wasn't enough, he added that the stuff was mostly mail. Royal Mail, once loaded, could not be offloaded, according to the traffic manual. 'Don't bet on it', I said.

I called the fleet manager. Needless to say, he was not available. I settled for the duty officer. 'Get a message to him', I said. 'Get authority to offload excess cargo, including mail at Shannon, and get a signal to me there. Get all this down in your log'. He promised and I heard no more. I didn't expect to. I knew that in Shannon, if I made it, there would be no problem.

We left on schedule and headed for Shannon. The weather reports were unhelpful, wavering around limits, but the guy in the tower was cheerful and besides, he knew the BOAC limits. I flew a very tidy instrument approach and we landed at Shannon. I knew I had it made, confidence in me had risen all round. I could reach out and touch it.

In Shannon they were just as anxious to see me away as I was to be off. They off loaded the excess mail without demur. I went to the Met. office where the midnight charts were being prepared. They were anxious to know if I wanted one; the revised forecasts would be available shortly. I looked at the

Captain Jeff Gray, BOAC.

spacing of the isobars and declined the offer. 'If you don't mind', I said, 'I'll stick with the 18h00 and stay with my present flight plan, and be away as soon as the refuelling is complete'. 'Take some thing for the wife and kids, Captain', the forecaster advised. I took a walk out to the aeroplane. There was no need to pass on the forecaster's advice. The engineers had already erred on the heavy-handed side. We cranked up and lumbered out across the field, meticulous in our checks and responses. The old Stratocruiser got airborne somewhere near the runway's end, more by virtue of the earth's curvature than anything else. We were off and running.

At longitude 30° west we were looking good, on time and up on fuel. Gander weather was holding up. The navigator was gloomy. 'That bloke in Shannon was probably right, Jeff. I expect that low to move to where he'd got it, that will tighten the gradient, increase the component, you'll need strong nerves'. He tapered off. 'Still', he said, 'if that's right, it should keep Gander clear'.

We droned on towards the point of no return. I reviewed the situation, then went back and found the supervisory captain to tell him the decision. 'It's all yours, Jeff', he said, and went back to sleep. The navigator was right. The headwind increased, eating away the margins. It still looked pretty good to me. At this late stage we could afford the punishment. We would have

Gander, with Stephenville as an alternative and the actuals were holding nicely and I had never hoped for more than that at any stage. We landed in Gander and refuelled, 16 hours and 19 minutes into the flight and only the last stage down the eastern seaboard to come. I loaded up with extra fuel, just for the sheer luxury of it and headed for Idlewild. Five hours and thirty-eight minutes later we were on the chocks in New York.

The shuttle flight to Bermuda posed no serious problem, nor did the return to the UK. I was home in time for Christmas, opening presents and eating plum pudding on the same day as everyone else. The supervisory captain gave me the best present of all. 'Keep that up', he said. 'You'll have no problems'.

During most of this period we were blessed with a decent chairman, Sir Miles Thomas. Of all the many chairmen, before and since, he was, perhaps, the only one who made the effort to get to know his staff and to encourage them by imparting a sense of loyalty and cohesion. BOAC have had more chairmen than most people have had hot dinners. Sir Miles was the only one I can recall seeing or meeting. He was a self-publicist, which was no bad thing in his position, as by this method he also brought publicity to the airline. During his tenure of office he made a real attempt to tidy things up. He reduced staff numbers drastically without too much heartache and he reorganised the fleets. Although the company was still heavily in the red, on finding that the deficits were reducing he even managed to raise pay.

During his reign, most of the runners from the Brabazon stable were put out to graze; and a sorry lot they turned out to be, either baulking or falling at the first fence or, plagued by some fatal defect, failing to stay the course. The Hermes had their fairly brief run on the African routes and were sold off to the accompaniment of an industrial dispute with the maintenance engineers. The Tudor, in its various versions, did at last acquit itself on the Berlin airlift but when that was over it faded into oblivion. Although tracing its descent from the most successful of the wartime bombers, the Lancaster, it was plagued by performance and aerodynamic shortcomings.

It killed its chief designer, Roy Chadwick, when he went up for a test flight. During assembly the aileron controls had been crossed and the machine crashed.

The two giant airliners, the Bristol Brabazon land plane and the Saunders Roe Princess flying boat were both quietly scrapped without ever seeing airline service. Both suffered due to their size and weight from the lack of suitable engines to power them. Existing engines were coupled together – some said, cobbled together – to get them airborne. Years of trials and tests followed before they were led off to the aviation equivalent of the knacker's yard.

The turboprops had more success and indeed, the small Viscount was a winner and a bestseller, alone, perhaps, of all the British airliners. The Britannia, of direct interest to BOAC, was made the centre of the most determined sales and publicity campaign.

As we went about our business in North America, newly converted Britannia crews were everywhere flying route familiarisation flights and demonstrations, and generally enjoying the experience and the unaccustomed luxury of the cash allowances thrust upon them wherever they went. It was all to no avail. The airline customers held back and BOAC alone, apart from El Al, put the aircraft into service. It was really a very fine machine and, aside from the serious engine icing problems that only then came to light, it deserved a better run than it had.

The first one I saw in actual service passed above me around 15° west as we both headed for London into the lightening eastern sky. Against the dramatic backcloth of the dawn, his condensation trail unfurled gleaming red and gold, gradually narrowing down as he sped away from us. The Stratocruiser was suddenly queen no longer. All too soon, however, the Britannia herself was overtaken as the new generation of jet-powered aeroplanes were rolled out. The first of these had appeared early. The Comet entered service in May 1952 and, exactly a year later, the first failure occurred. Generally speaking, the British build things on a massive scale, 'like a brick shit house'.

British aeroplanes usually come within this category, but not so the Comet. It was lightly built, unfortunately too light to withstand the repeated demands of pressurising the hull and the term, 'metal fatigue' entered the language. Few aviators were happy with the enquiry into the first Comet disaster at Calcutta. It was said that the aeroplane had broken up on flying into a thunderstorm. Certainly, Calcutta is a place where thunderstorms of the most violent variety abound. Certainly, too, on departure it is difficult at times to avoid them, even equipped with weather radar, when the scope for manoeuvre is limited. And we all knew that a really violent thunderstorm could produce forces sufficient to break up an aeroplane, especially if given a little assistance from the pilot by being over-controlling. The verdict was, however, just a little too easy, too convenient and it assumed a little too much to be convincing.

It was some time before the second and third disasters occurred. Early the next year, near Elba, a second Comet split asunder, spilling its human and other contents into the Mediterranean, and a third completed the hat trick near Rome in April. Apart from the dreadful losses occasioned by these disasters, the fleet had to be grounded and with it, a major part of BOAC ground to a halt. Arrangements were hastily made for chartered aircraft to operate some routes and second-hand aeroplanes, to be bought in under these most unfavourable conditions to keep the airline afloat. I think Sir Miles did a pretty good job under the circumstances, but it was a major setback.

The investigations at Farnborough laid bare the problems, and aviation knowledge and construction methods were greatly changed as a result. Redesigned and rebuilt Comets came back into service in the nick of time to usher in the jet age. The Stratocruisers were relegated to a lower division and ended their time on the West Africa run. The regulars on that route were torn between believing that, at last, they were being provided with the best the Corporation could provide or that they were being given the cast-offs from more commercially important routes. The Stratocruiser itself didn't much care for its new environment. Those massive piston engines with their four banks of cylinders didn't like the high temperatures. In particular, the rear bank, starved of a cooling airflow by the three banks ahead of them, was prone to overheating and, near the ground at low speeds, the cowl gills had to be opened a long way to keep the cylinder head temperatures out of the red or, at least, not too far into the red. You have to be realistic about such things. There was no merit in taking off from Kano, for example, on a hot day with the cowl gills well open and all the temperatures within range, if by so doing, the immense drag thus created cut back on performance after take-off, to the extent that you wouldn't have been able to sustain an engine failure and live to tell the tale. The best you could do was level off about one thousand feet above the ground and accelerate to get more airflow through the engine and get the cowls closed down before climbing away. If we didn't know much about temperature inversions when we started, we soon did.

The truth of the matter was that we had seen the ultimate in the development of the piston engine and the propeller and come to the end of that road. Frank Whittle's baby, the jet engine, although in its infancy, opened up the way ahead.

The jet age

There is an old adage about teaching old dogs new tricks. This was what aviation now had to do. In moving from the propeller-driven aeroplanes to the jets there was more to learn than we knew. The start of the jet age was marked by what has subsequently been called 'learning errors'.

I was transferred, with the retirement of the Stratocruisers, to the Comet fleet and so went back to the eastern routes. A great many things had happened while I'd been away. The process of dismantling the British Empire was, by now, well advanced and gathering speed. I found myself, because of my junior status, on the long haul down to Australia. Even at the new cruising speeds in the Comet which can achieve three-quarters of the speed of sound (Mach 0.76), Australia was a long way off. The trips were very long, with large changes of time zone and climate and were deservedly the most unpopular, reserved almost exclusively for junior captains. Let me say straight away that I loved Australia. It was love at first sight. When I set foot on the tarmac at Darwin and went ashore, the first official I met was the medic, examining health documents. I think he was surprised by my youthful appearance. 'Good to see some new blood and younger captains coming along in the old BOAC', he said. I was at once flattered and made to feel welcome. They followed this up by producing the first decent cup of tea I'd had since leaving England. If I hadn't been convinced already, that did it. I liked the Aussies at once and nothing that has happened since has changed that view.

When 1 got to Melbourne in my little Comet we were accommodated at the Menzies Hotel. I awoke the next morning to the sound of horse-drawn transport in the street and, from afar came the unmistakable sound of a tramcar. It seemed reminiscent of early morning in a northern city, Aberdeen or Edinburgh perhaps, with milk being delivered and the first of the workers' trams screeching its way towards the city centre.

I arose refreshed and dressed and wandered off downstairs to locate the dining room. The day starts early in Melbourne and breakfast was being served. 'I'll have the lamb's fry', I said. It came with everything; a mixed grill of eggs and sausage, bacon and lamb's fry, enough for a regiment. When I'd finished I walked to the street door, the hall porter stood there gazing out into the street surveying his domain. 'Morning Skipper', he said, 'what do you think of Melbourne?' We Europeans are not accustomed to being recognised. Only celebrities expect to be recognised. It took a moment for this to sink in. I told him that it had reminded me, for just a moment, of my boyhood, when I might have thought myself transported in time and place. My plans, I told him, included a visit to the town hall to see if there was a concert there that night as I'd heard of their famous state orchestra. 'Then', I said, 'The Yarra, I'll have to see that, and that will do for starters'. He seemed inclined to chat. 'All the aviators, when they come to Melbourne, come here and stay at the Menzies'. He mentioned one or two legendary names and I looked at him keenly to see if he was taking the mickey in including me in such exalted company. But no, clearly aviators came lumped together in his book. When he was a junior, just a lad really, he'd gone out with the others into the throng in the street to rescue Amy Johnson and help carry her, shoulder high, into the foyer. We looked up and down the empty street, he hearing and seeing scenes from the past, while I struggled to imagine what it must have looked and sounded like.

When I walked away towards the city centre, towards the sounds of the tram cars, I had to turn my mind to the sights and sounds of the day and away from the imagined tumult and excitement conjured up by a hall porter.

There were drawbacks to the Australian route. Homeward bound one trip, I'd got as far as Bombay, when the ground engineers downed tools and declared a strike. As no aeroplanes were dispatched from London, no more arrived down route. The strike dragged on. Bombay was experiencing one of its wettest and most persistent monsoons. Although it is an interesting enough place, even Bombay begins to pall after two weeks of very wet weather and with each passing day we became more bored. Bombay had prohibition at that time and, eventually, we applied for liquor permits. In order to join the other foreign residents and be issued with a licence, it was necessary to sign a form declaring oneself to be an alcoholic and 'ordinarily accustomed to consuming foreign liquors'. I liked the crafty language, 'foreign liquors'. We found the stuff was all Indian-made and quite horrible. The 'foreign liquors' had to be consumed in permit rooms. These were unpleasant places located in each major hotel. A customs officer sat at one end of the bar crossing off coupons from the licences. There was one cheerful aspect. If you produced a blank unused permit and made sure everyone knew about it, you didn't have to pay for the drinks. All manner of new-found friends, already seated at the bar, were only too delighted to do so.

When the strike was over, the services had to be restarted and, before you could say Jack Robinson I found myself heading east again back to Australia. Rosters promised that they would turn us around again just as soon as they could. We got home six weeks after we had first set out.

Every nation has developed its own legislation and set of rules governing civil aviation within its airspace. Although the International Civil Aviation Organisation in Montreal has done a great deal to unify procedures and regulations, the airline captain has, perforce, to know his stuff before operating through other territories. This is particularly true of Australia.

Just as the Australian continent developed its own particular flora and fauna in isolation from the rest of the world, to a very much smaller degree they appeared to do the same thing in aviation, developing rules which were sometimes at variance with other countries. But the chief difference lies in the Australian attitude to rules and regulations. If you are deceived by the Australian attitude towards life, that Jack's as good as his master, the assumption of equality and the bluff 'hail fellow well met' attitude into thinking that he is careless of rules and authority, you could hardly be more wrong. In aviation, the Australians are sticklers for rules, and their application. It is

A light-hearted moment on the flight deck of a Comet 4. Jeff Gray is on the right.

the Brit, in fact who takes the rules lightly, but not for long, not in Australia that is. I am a great admirer of this diligent, and meaningful application. It's no good having rules if they are impracticable or if they are not applied. Down under they have to be both.

I learnt about this very early on. In Sydney one night, with the briefing procedure completed for the flight to Darwin, I submitted my flight plan. It was refused. Air traffic control pointed out that the weather forecast for my destination expired before my time of arrival. There was only half an hour in it, but I had to go back to the Met. office and have the forecast extended before I could proceed. The actual point itself was trivial but the principle immensely important. This attitude underlies the Australian approach to aviation.

At that time, the airways routes within Australia were equipped with a thing called VAR. The technicalities are not important. It was an intermediate stage between the old low frequency radio ranges and the later, very high frequency omni-directional ranges. Perhaps the government had been too quick off the mark in ordering the equipment and had got stuck with it. It had appeared briefly in the USA but was not used for long and was soon superseded. In Australia, it remained in use for years and was indeed, very practical, but was unfamiliar to newcomers. At this stage in our affairs, the Corporation, not unsympathetically, agreed that the trips were just too long to be endured and arranged for crews to be posted down under for three-monthly periods to cover the end of the route. From being the most unpopular route, the Aussie one at once became the most popular. Everyman and his dog wanted in. We junior captains were kept busy for a time in clearing newcomers to the route.

Now the Comet had a very fine instrument system or flight director, built by Smiths in the UK but it has one drawback. Under certain circumstances, when flying away from a station the system had to be rotated through 180 degrees, so that the pictorial display was reversed and the user had to stand on his head mentally to follow the display. When the system was combined with the VAR it therefore had its limitations and difficulty.

Down at Melbourne at the old airport of Essendon, one overshoot procedure involved proceeding to a holding point called Diggers' Rest, which was at the intersection of two separate VAR radials. As a little 'passing out' exercise on the route clearance, I would ask newcomers to give me the details of how to set up the Smiths' system for the correct pictorial presentation of the Diggers' Rest hold. From the start of the overshoot to reaching the hold would take about two and a half minutes' flight time and some of that would be used in carrying out other drills and checks. I awarded no points or prizes for a correct answer, nor did the signing of the clearance form depend in any way upon it. This was just as well. Usually we had got to Singapore and the room balcony of Raffles Hotel before they arrived at the correct solution. In fairness to the Australians, I don't believe they had taken up the Smiths flight director system.

So what were the new tricks that the old dogs had to learn? Some of them were self-evident and well known, and in the conversion courses and training they were put across well enough. But the trainers, in fact, knew little more (perhaps even less) than the line pilots and we had, perforce, to find out together, the hard way, down the routes.

A battle developed over the cruise–climb technique. The earlier

Comets had severe shortcomings in range and performance. Some very clever techniques and dodges had been developed to compensate for these. Maximum range and economy could be achieved in the cruise, for example, by setting the engine power for the altitude and then, as fuel was burnt off and weight reduced, allowing the aeroplane to find its own cruising height, in what theoretically would be a long and very slow climb or increase in altitude. The aeroplane thus occupied a band of altitudes, waffling about there at, or close to, its performance ceiling and perilously close to what later became known as coffin corner. Fortunately it wasn't a critical aeroplane in any respect and was free of vices, otherwise there might well have been some interesting runaway situations or 'jet upsets' as they became called. The hired hands knew no more about this than their smarter brothers at base but it was immediately evident that the cruise–climb technique was impracticable, apart from any feelings of insecurity engendered by the sensation of hanging on a sky-hook. With one aeroplane in a cruise–climb down the Persian Gulf and another proceeding in the opposite direction, insisting on the same procedure, such air traffic control as existed there was hard put to it to make sure they avoided each other. In parts of the world where air traffic control existed in name only, it looked not only stupid but dangerous, as the high flying traffic increased.

The line pilots abandoned cruise–climb and adopted instead a level cruise, climbing in steps when the reduced weight permitted clearance to the next, higher level. The Corporation continued to pressurise the pilots into cruise–climb, going so far as to write to the air traffic control authorities requesting them to insist on clearances involving cruise–climb.

A puzzled air traffic controller called me from Bahrain when I refused the proffered cruise–climb. What was he to do? My company were writing and insisting on cruise–climb? 'Leave them to fly their desks', I said. 'Be guided by the line pilots, they fly the aeroplanes'. As the traffic increased, cruise–climb fell out of use and disappeared from the language.

In case what I have written appears to claim that all the wisdom resides in the line pilot, I must hasten to correct the impression. Not so. He is, however, the first to know of any operational problem and has, perforce, to accommodate to it and feed his knowledge back to base where, with greater resources and knowledge, better solutions can be found. The system works only up to a point and the pilots have been far too tolerant of its deficiencies, using unsuitable aerodromes, making do with inadequate equipment and covering up shortcomings. When the inevitable happens and something gets bent, they become very indignant on hearing the verdict, 'pilot error'. No one understands them. Then why hadn't they said or done something beforehand?

A little cloud appeared to mar the otherwise blue skies of the Comet fleet. A sequence of incidents began, usually involving an unexpected and unplanned contact with the ground. This was very worrying. As far apart as Madrid and Nairobi, Rome and Calcutta, aeroplanes were crashing down through treetops, usually on the approach to land. In one such incident, it was reported, the aeroplane hit a tree on the approach, overshot and made another attempt, only to hit the self-same tree at the second attempt. People were landing at the wrong aerodromes. There appeared to be no common factor. All manner of theories were advanced. The Ministry of Civil Aviation made one of their very rare interventions in the Corporation's affairs. Flight inspectors descended upon us from the Strand. They sat in on every base check. The list of failures grew as the training captains, thus observed, applied the rules with absolute rigidity.

'Tash' Robbie was the first to break the sequence and score a first-time pass under this new regime. When he learned that he'd been taken off his forthcoming scheduled roster prior to undergoing his competency check, his moustache fairly bristled, and those responsible got the benefit of the sharp edge of his tongue. It was, of course, very much tongue in cheek on his part. The Ministry's solution was to subject all the pilots to an additional base check under the supervision of their own inspectors as far as possible and an additional line check too. This worked like a charm. The incidents stopped. I am still at a loss to explain it. Perhaps each man, thus examined, was forced in turn to examine his own performance and application and discipline and take greater care.

Ye canna be too careful

Captain Donald Anderson of North Atlantic fame was heard to say, on more than one occasion, 'Ye canna be too careful!' Although this has been more elegantly expressed such as 'Eternal vigilance is the price of safety', I much prefer Donald's version. Throughout civil aviation it is important to remember that it is the passenger who pays the wages and, whatever immediate masters you may have in the airline and the government authorities, it is the fare-paying passenger who has the say.

Fare-paying passenger may be forgiven for thinking that there are times when the airline staff have lost sight of this great truth. However, there are times when the passengers can be a damned nuisance and, even, let it be said, worse; a menace to themselves and all on board. The drunken passenger comes within this last category. Ships' crews are notoriously bad travellers. When positioning by air between ports, they invariably drink too much and are thoroughly unpleasant traveling companions as a result.

But the most memorable case in my experience concerned a fellow captain. When my crew and I reached the airport in readiness to meet the incoming flight, a signal was passed through air traffic control asking for the joining captain to meet the aircraft immediately on arrival. No reason was given for the request. We were in Bahrain in the Persian Gulf and no better means of drawing attention or arousing curiosity could have been devised as, by the time I got the signal, everyone on the island knew about it. It must be something very unusual to signal ahead in so mysterious a fashion and the thought of a hijacker or some security risk came to mind, as the worldwide hijacking season was, by now, in full swing.

I dismissed the thought and made my way out to the tarmac to await the arrival. I borrowed the ground engineer's headset so that I could plug myself into the intercom as soon as the aircraft came on chocks, without the need to fight my way on board against the stream.

The incoming captain was newly promoted and was having a problem with two drunks. He proposed leaving them to me. 'I don't want them', I said. 'Have them turfed off. A night in an Arab jail will work wonders for them'. But there was a further problem, apparently. One of the drunks was a senior BOAC captain dead-heading to Singapore. The senior captain and his travelling companion had been fighting in the first class cabin. Well, not exactly fighting, more like wrestling on the floor, among the other passengers.

'Were they', I ventured, 'indulging in a trial of strength, do you think?' 'Yes, that kind of thing'. 'Ah', I said, 'I have it, I know who it is. Leave it with me, then, and, whatever you do, don't go making voyage reports, and don't send any more daft signals. Make up some silly story to satisfy the curiosity of the locals'. The captain's playmate was disembarking in Bahrain and looked as if he might just make it unaided. So that was half the problem solved. When the opportunity arose, I went back to see my friend. He struggled to recognise me and made an effort to say a big hello. I moved on as soon as I could to see the other passengers and judge their reactions. I decided that Morpheus was about to overcome him and nothing needed to be done. I instructed the steward to give my friend a couple of stiff ones if he showed any sign of wanting more, and knock him out cold. 'Don't get into any hand grips or trials of strength with him', I advised. We proceeded with the flight.

When we had transited Calcutta and were approaching the coast of Burma, with the day far advanced, the steward came forward to report that my friend was stirring. 'Tell him where we are', I said. 'Tell him we're approaching Phuket. That'll locate him for sure, and tell him I want to see him on the flight deck pronto'. When the steward had queried the place name and the pronunciation, he went off to do as bidden, but his face expressed uncertainty.

The First Officer leant across and looked at me anxiously. 'Taking a bit of a risk, Skipper', he said. 'Supposing someone reports it and it all comes out, you'll be in the fertiliser!' 'Never mind', I replied, 'there are times when you have to do these things, you've got to look after your mates when you can'.

I became involved in the security business very early on, before most people were aware of it. It happened this way. In late November 1964 I was due to start an eastern trip. The phone rang earlier that day and the roster clerk told me of the changes. I was to turn around in Singapore and return with a charter flight. The charter itself started from Nairobi. I was to position the aeroplane across from Singapore. 'OK', I said, 'but what about the nav gear?'

Apparently it wasn't possible for the navigation equipment bag to be got ready in time, it would be sent on to Singapore by a later flight. 'There's one more snag', I said, 'I doubt if the aeroplane can get across the oggin in one move, I'll need a refuelling stop. Colombo, I suppose, or better still, from the range point of view, in Gan. You know, that little island stuck out there in the Indian Ocean? The RAF have a base there. If you'd look it up for me, get all the details, I'd be obliged'.

The support services in BOAC were always first rate and I thought it unlikely that they would let me down. The navigation gear and all the stuff I needed would undoubtedly get to Singapore in good time.

It did, however, cross my mind that the RAF in Changi would have a more first-hand information about their base in Gan and so, when I got to Singapore, I made it my business to go along and see them. They were most courteous and helpful. It was a good thing I went, as the navigation bag never did arrive but, armed with all the information I needed, we set course cheerfully for Gan, the home of those intrepid navigators and seamen of the Maldives. It was home, also, for a small RAF station staff on one-year postings for, although they were picturesque and idyllic, the islands did have their limitations. There was only one white woman on the island, who was a nursing sister in the Princess Mary's Royal Air Force Nursing Service.

I had a list of all the radio frequencies for the area, which didn't help very much, as the radio gear was crystal-controlled and could not be altered without having the appropriate crystals. It's going to be a quiet trip, I thought, with nobody to talk to on the way across. And so it proved. When we had run out of range of Singapore and Madras, we had no further contact with air traffic control until we were within sight of the east coast of Africa. This was not as bad as it seems, the high frequency network is notoriously erratic in nature and whole sectors over parts of Africa and the Far East may have to be flown without the benefit of radio communications to this very day. So we plugged along cheerfully.

The transit stop in Gan was most interesting and yet completely uneventful. The whole station was beautifully kept, the briefing rooms a model of tidiness and order, the gravel paths linking them were raked and the stones marking the edges were of uniform size and each one was carefully whitewashed. We even met the one white woman there and chatted awhile. An aircraft arrival was the highlight of everyone's day and civilian flights were rare but, having no passengers, we were to prove a bit of a disappointment, so the people who had come to meet us drifted away again.

We reached Nairobi without incident. It was then that we learned the reason for the charter flight. The very last of the British troops were formally taking their farewell of Kenya and we were to fly them out. On the very day of their departure a snag arose. The African nations that we had to overfly on our flight refused permission. So there we were at the last minute, all fuelled up and nowhere to go.

I consulted my school atlas. It seemed to me that we could make Aden without overflying any of these sensitive chaps and, as we still had a British garrison there, would be assured of a welcome. We also had a service to Aden and there would be a crew there. What then, was the question? A long flight from Aden, around the Arabian peninsula up the gulf to Bahrain then, if not direct to the UK, a refuelling stop at Istanbul would do it. There would be slip crews in both places, so with any luck it should work. I had them bash off the necessary signals and got to work on flight planning the sector to Aden. Meantime the troops arrived at the airfield and I missed all the foot-stamping on the tarmac and the running up and down of flags, but we were all ready in time for boarding and the last of the British garrison left on time.

When we arrived at Aden, the slip crew were on the tarmac to greet us, ready to take over. They had accepted the change of plan without demur and, by this time, Headquarters were back in the picture and had agreed it with one of their 'firstly, secondly, thirdly' signals. So, firstly, the slip crew in Aden were to take over the charter flight. Secondly, the incoming crew would remain in Aden and operate flight so-and-so in their stead, then thirdly, the slip crew in Bahrain etc. etc. To my surprise, the joining crew seemed quite cheerful about the new arrangements and were pleased to make the change over. We were handed a bag of nails. The flight we were to operate from Aden was being sent specially to fetch the colonial secretary, (Anthony Greenwood) who was in Aden on a tour of inspection. On the previous day the 'rebels' had, unsuccessfully, tried to blow him up. It was thought likely that they would continue their endeavours and the aeroplane sent to take him back would, naturally, be a target for their attention.

The British in Aden were not doing well. They were under pressure from the locals, who had taken up arms against them to throw them out and were under pressure from their political masters in London, who appeared undecided as to whether to stop and fight or pack up and go. This gave them the worst of both worlds with no clear directives as to what they were to do; only what they were not to do.

I had seen the break up of the British Empire proceeding stage by stage in many countries and, frankly, I shed no tears for the barren rocks of Aden. I could not but feel sorry for the troops there caught in such a quandary. My immediate concern, however, had to be with the outbound flight; to do all I could to see that we did not fall prey to the bombers. The military washed their hands of us. They had handed the colonial secretary back to the Civil Authority and his security was no longer their concern. I was disappointed. After some agitation, I got the manager of Aden Airways to call a conference to discuss the departure. This was achieved only by making it plain that, unless what we now call strict security was observed, the flight wasn't going anywhere. We put our heads together with all the departments immediately concerned with the flight and came up with a plan.

I wanted to limit the number of people involved in handling the aircraft and thus, the risk of unauthorised packages finding their way aboard. The services supplied were to be kept to an absolute minimum. We should need fuel, one tanker crew would have to be vetted, and no other person permitted near. Engineering staff would not go near, and the flight engineer would carry out the essential servicing and sign the aircraft out. By essential, I meant counting the engines and kicking the tyres. No catering or stores could be allowed. The flight must bring in whatever was needed, or do without. Mail and freight would be accepted as usual, but would drive on past the aeroplane and be parked in a spare dispersal until after we had left. Only passengers known to the airline would be accepted and all would be searched. I would look in to see how this was being done. If I was satisfied, I would accept them; if not, they would join their baggage in the spare dispersal. Happy, at length, that I'd got some sense into them, I went back to the hostelry to brief my crew.

Either I mishandled the crew briefing or I had misjudged them, for it went awry on me. One stewardess decided that it was not for her; she wanted out. I had to drop my usual easy-going pose and let it be known that she could opt out: in fact I'd be happy to suspend her straight away. She'd be off-loaded, of course, and when she could return to the UK I couldn't say: that would be her problem. This stopped the rot abruptly. We were then able to get down to cases, particularly our own suitcases, and how to safeguard them against interference, particularly in a hotel open to the public where any one of the staff could be sympathetic to the 'terrorists'.

The next day we cracked off early for the airport and, to my astonishment, things went reasonably close to plan. Even so, I was uneasily aware that you cannot be entirely secure in the complex business of turning an aircraft around. Opportunity for a determined attacker would certainly exist. But for a first time and a one-off operation, it wasn't bad and the Aden Airways manager seemed both pleased and surprised when I said so. As we climbed away into the blue skies heading for Cairo, the tower operator came through to say he had just received the message I had anticipated: that we had a bomb on board and what was he to say? 'Like I told you', I said, 'tell them to get stuffed!'.

My involvement with Aden did not end there. As time went by it became apparent that political considerations effectively prevented military action and on successive, if fortunately infrequent visits, I noticed that the insurgents had tightened their grip on the airport. The sound of mortar fire, only faintly heard on one visit, sounded just beyond the perimeter on a later one. Oil drums filled with water and some with sand appeared on the tarmac, arranged, hopefully, to provide some protection for the aeroplanes and the people working around them against shrapnel and stray bullets. Clearly the days of the British on the barren rocks of Aden were numbered. It was also evident that there was a deal of dissent among the garrison; some strongly favouring an all-out effort to defeat the locals and remain in Aden, others, on the other hand, accepting what appeared to be the British government's line of gradual withdrawal and defeat. The governor was thought to be in the former camp and not to be altogether in sympathy with his political masters. However, it was decided that he would retire and it fell to me to bring him home. Our route to Aden at that time was through Khartoum. We had long since given up slipping in Aden, using Khartoum instead, although this made a lengthy trip of it, with a long lay-over in Sudan because of the infrequent services. On the flight across from Khartoum to

Aden I turned my attention to the matter of flags and flagpoles.

BOAC had, early on in its existence, got into the business of flying the flag. This, of course, could only be done while on the ground, for obvious reasons. It didn't present much of a problem on earlier aeroplanes as flag holders could be mounted outside the pilot's direct vision window and within easy reach. The flying of flags is not the simple, straightforward business it might appear to be at first sight. In a nation with as much experience of flags as the British, it has become hemmed in by tradition and usage and it had been thought necessary to provide a briefing sheet on the subject for the crews.

I was fairly well up on the subject as, in the early days of BOAC on the Yorks we did a great deal of flag waving. It was customary then, to stick the Union Jack out of the captain's window in the superior port position and the local flag, if any, out of the starboard. Where the territory being visited didn't run to its own flag, as it shared the British one, special rules applied and the house flag, or even the Civil Aviation flag could be flown. If, in the case of VIPs, they were entitled to fly their own standard, great care had to be taken to get it right as people in this category can be very sensitive and, instead of being pleased and flattered by such courtesies, they become indignant and readily offended if you get it muddled, flying their flag in inferior positions, or whatever.

As aeroplanes became faster and more complicated with pressurised hulls, it fortunately became more difficult to fly the flags from them and the practice began to die out. On the VC10s, perhaps the very last modern aeroplane to make such provision, the sextant mounting in the cockpit roof had been adapted for the mounting of flags. It was a complicated matter. The tiny roof hatch, operated by Bowden cable, had been intended to accept the periscopic part of a specially designed sextant. To stick flags and flagpoles through it without damage, and to remember to remove them and close up the hatch again before flight required a little care and, of course, in the pressure of departure, particularly with VIPs, items not ordinarily on the check list can easily be forgotten.

So it was that I read the briefing sheet carefully and, with a pen, amended the check list for departure while otherwise unoccupied on the way across. Nothing could have been simpler. There was only the Union Jack to fly and it had already been thoughtfully provided, mounted on its staff and carefully furled so that it would go through the small periscopic hatch. Great.

The British authorities in Aden had decided that Governor Turnbull was one of its favourite sons and, whether it was because they wished to express their agreement with his views or merely to mark the occasion, or for sheer brotherly love, they had decided to make an occasion of it. As we sat there on the tarmac completing the outbound arrangements and having the fuel topped up, not without difficulty, as everyone seemed to be involved elsewhere, we could see the troops parading up and down. Bands played, soldiers were marching past in salute, flights of aeroplanes flew overhead and ceremonial guns boomed out. Always a sucker for a parade, I was sorry to miss it and not give it my full attention.

Eventually, it came to our turn. We had overcome all the difficulties and looked as if we would be ready in good time. Senior officers and officials began to gather and line up by the aircraft steps preparatory to bidding the Governor farewell. I instructed the flight engineer as to his flag-raising duties, having decided that, as soon as we saw the cavalcade approaching, he was to stuff the flag pole through the periscopic hatch, turning it in the appropriate direction for the appropriate number of turns to ensure that it unfurled. The moment for action came and I sat comfortably in my seat, looking down on the scene below. My attention was caught by a senior naval officer, much decorated and heavily encrusted with gold braid, as is the Navy habit. He, I felt sure, had seen the flag appear and unfurl, and something in his expression told me all was not well. I turned to my crew to ask them if any of them had been Boy Scouts in their youth. Apparently none of them had. 'Would any of you know if a Union Jack was mounted upside down?', I asked. Apparently not. I asked the engineer to take the flag in so that

I could inspect it. He carefully turned it again to furl the flag around its pole and, following the directions precisely, the flag was brought in. Sure enough, it was upside down. Moreover, it was firmly stitched to its lanyard so that it couldn't be reversed. The lanyard could be upended, thus getting the flag the right way up, but leaving it then at half mast. I wasn't sure that this would be appropriate and so I ordered the wretched thing be put back into its stowage. I could see that it wasn't a new flag and had spent all its life to date being flown upside down. We closed the hatch and got on with the business in hand.

It is of the utmost importance to VIPs that they arrive at their destination precisely at the time arranged. That makes it all the more curious that they are notoriously neglectful of departing on time, The one is so contingent upon the other that it hardly needs stressing. Getting them away on time requires a special skill and technique. Right at the very last stage, faced with the hand-shaking and goodbyes at the foot of the aircraft steps, is a great danger point. The less experienced VIP is bound to fall for it and embark on another impromptu speech, instead of embarking on the aircraft steps. I had, by now, devised my own method of dealing with this. I would call for number four engine, on the far side of the aeroplane to be started up. If the banshee wail of a jet engine starting up proved insufficient to deafen the listeners and cut off the speech-making, when number four was alight, it would become necessary to open it up a little to supply air to the number three and so get that started. This technique never failed and it didn't on this occasion, either. We rolled off the chocks to an on-time departure. As we climbed away and checked through 10,000 feet preparatory to changing frequency to the area control, the tower operator asked if we had remembered to take the flag down. 'Yes', I assured him, we had got that bit right. He wished us the traditional happy landings and signed off. I knew then that the story of the upside down Union Jack had got across the airfield and as far as the control tower already.

It was said that in Culkins on Third Avenue, in the Golden Bar in Beirut and in similar places where the cognoscenti were wont to gather, if you desired to get anywhere in the management of BOAC you first had to draw attention to yourself and this was best achieved by 'bending' one. Not too seriously of course, just enough to get noticed. Joining the Freemasons was another route and, if the two were combined, it was almost certain to lead on to fame. The line pilot remained critical of those who directed their affairs. Management at fleet level had changed and current practising captains had been appointed to such offices. They flew the line and managed on a part-time basis and, as pilot/management was our baby and the British Airline Pilots' Association (BALPA) had pushed hard for it, so we remained hopeful of a great improvement in our affairs.

To my mind, we proved that '*plus ça change, plus c'est la même chose*'.[1] Certainly management were more approachable and perhaps more understanding, but maybe we expected too much of them in our isolation. At the time we had a splendid fleet manager in Cliff Alabaster, a grand little aeroplane in the Comet, an interesting route to fly, if a trifle long, and a cheerful, extrovert bunch of guys for company. It was a good time and better was to come.

A grand strategy had been laid down for BOAC, whereby we flew the trunk routes, calling at the major gateways, and feeder services brought passengers to these gates. All the smaller airlines in which the Corporation had an interest, or which it owned outright, the associated companies, were to play their part in this grand design. The Comet service from Hong Kong was named the Cannonball and offered the most direct and rapid flight from the colony to the UK. However, as the British Empire was dismembered and each and every state felt itself freed and independent, high on their list of symbols of their new-found independence was a national airline. New and rival airlines sprang up to fly alongside established carriers and the feeder concept never really got off the ground. The Comet was losing out against growing competition as bigger and faster jets took to the air; but better was to come in the VC10.

Towards the end of the Comet's life, it was apparent that it had

1 The more things change, the more they remain the same.

become outclassed and outmoded and its popularity rapidly waned. To comply with the new loading fingers which were appearing, the Corporation decided to change the passenger loading procedure, by bringing them in through the front door. This door, unfortunately, led directly into the galley, which had to be disguised as far as possible before boarding. If the food larders were late in being returned, they had to be hastily stowed in the nearby lavatory to allow customers access. Following one departure the steward came to see me. 'I've got a passenger who insists on seeing you', he said. 'I can't pacify him, I'm afraid'. I enquired why. The passenger had arrived at the aeroplane in a state of acute discomfort. As soon as he got inside the galley he had demanded to know where the toilet was. Before the steward could answer, the passenger spotted it and made a beeline for the door. 'I'm sorry sir', cried the steward, 'you can't go in there'. The passenger took no heed and pushed the door open. He was confronted by the sight of stacked galley equipment. With relief so close and yet denied him, the passenger made a tremendous effort at self control. 'What the hell's all this?' he demanded. 'It's your dinner, sir!' said the steward, as indeed it was.

The VC10 was a splendid aeroplane from the pilot's and also the passengers' point of view. But it left a good deal to be desired in the layout of the galley, and the accountants saw it as a financial disaster. The Corporation got cold feet and tried to reduce their order for the plane. As the major and lead customer this did little to inspire confidence in the programme and blighted its sales prospects.

As a nationalised concern, the Company's affairs were prone to sudden shifts and changes of policy. When in power political parties appointed their own chaps to positions of authority both in the airline and the regulating bodies. It is a price, I suppose, that has to be paid by every state-owned concern. New brooms are always sweeping clean or trying, somehow, to leave their mark. On this occasion they left their mark all right, as scars on the aircraft manufacturing industry. The VC10 was to be the last serious commercial attempt by Britain to stay in the aircraft manufacturing business and sell to the world. It was doomed to failure, and only partly as a result of its cost. Plans for a larger version were quietly shelved.

On the routes it operated worldwide and, for the first time, crews were being cleared for worldwide operations. The Boeing 707s that the Corporation had purchased and operated at the same time were just as successful as the VC10 and, in the longer term, probably more so. But not in the eyes of the VC10 crews. It wasn't necessary to tell us that we mustn't criticise, as in the Hermes days: rather the reverse. These were, for me, the salad days, the best times and the coming of age of civil aviation.

There is, I suppose, a period in every man's life when he has achieved some small measure of success and security and reached a plateau based on maturity and experience and is still young enough to enjoy life. The airline captain in his forties is such a man. In addition, it seemed to me, we were at last being equipped with aeroplanes that were designed and fit for task and that the days of 'coming in on a wing and a prayer' were over. Air traffic control in most parts of the world was well established, leaving only a few nasties where, because of poor communication or lack of interest, we were still at risk. The jet engine, being a much simpler device than its predecessor with fewer moving parts, was more robust and reliable than earlier planes. The ground engineers were moving rapidly towards being able to pick up incipient engine failures on the ground, not in the air. Besides which, the aeroplanes themselves were over-engined or 'over-powered', so that the loss of one, even at the most critical stage of flight, could be safely managed. In navigation, long the Cinderella of aviation, Doppler was taking the guesswork out of it and inertial navigation was waiting in the wings to set us free from ground-based aids. At the terminals, precision approach aids were available to get us within sight of the runway on instruments, although it was already clear that the procedures and demands of instrument flying were taking human beings to the limits of their ability and skill and, as congestion grew, together with noise abatement procedures, standard approaches and departure procedures, restrictions and constraints of all kinds grew and multiplied. With the perversity of human nature, we took great pride in our ability to cope with these things, operating through the world's most congested and difficult airports. The increasing size of the aeroplanes, with increasing approach and landing speeds, demanded longer runways and, perhaps, because concrete is relatively cheap, longer runways were so constructed.

I found myself back on the Atlantic. The scene had changed dramatically. There were no longer problems of inadequate range, except on very rare occasions. The maritime airfields had fallen into disuse. The weather ships were being withdrawn. Weather satellites took pictures of the weather systems over the ocean for the met. men to pore over, and computers were being used to analyse the wind pattern and allocate tracks and flight levels across the ocean. Down the eastern seaboard of the USA and across the States generally, air traffic congestion had reached a dangerous pitch. Flights were becoming subject to lengthy arrival delays and, as some form of priority had to be given to the long-haul Atlantic traffic, the short-haul internal and Caribbean flights had to bear the brunt. To load up fuel to maximum landing weight, and over, became the norm. On several memorable occasions, New York's traffic was stacked along the seaboard from Miami to Newfoundland. The authorities were forced to react by buying new equipment, planning ahead and allocating slots, and opening up more gateways to the USA. Slowly and painfully they got around to it and the traffic congestion eased.

In New York itself they pulled down the elevated railway on Third Avenue and all the little shops, bars and restaurants that had flourished in its shadow disappeared when exposed to the bright sunlight, giving way to new offices and grand emporiums. The BOAC crews had to seek new pastures and meeting places. The need for the long lay-overs had gone as the crossing times were cut back to a comfortable seven hours or so. But into this peaceful scene of sunlit uplands appeared some discontent. The pilots had long been unhappy about their pay and their excursions to other lands and contact with others in the same business, who enjoyed far greater rewards, fostered their discontent. Led by a small group of vocal and determined individuals who, as elected BALPA officials, were willing to lay their heads on the block, a now or never attitude prevailed. The pilots were willing to strike in pursuit of their claims. The first attempt was not a complete success and had to be repeated. The airline ground to a halt, the pilots determined to have more money, the managers determined that they should not. Both sides were equally willing to damage their airline in pursuit of their aims.

A flight of mine ground to a halt in Nairobi. On arrival from Johannesburg, we were told that the strike was official. The aeroplane would be flown on to London and halted there. We proceeded to the Norfolk Hotel, as usual. In the morning the manager was apologetic. He would have to ask us to leave the Company rooms but he had other rooms. We settled for a most reasonable rate. The hotel manager wished to stay neutral. It was not his fight but, clearly, he knew that if he was to keep his business he had to keep the goodwill of his guests. We sat it out, the days passing pleasantly enough. There were several crews there. The chaps in Uganda phoned in, they weren't quite so well placed and I suggested that they move to Kenya if they could make it. Pilots from Kenya's East African Airways came around to see if they could help in any way. This was intended, and appreciated, most kindly, but they were nervous of becoming involved in any kind of dispute. Their nervousness was readily understood and we assured them that we lacked for nothing, which was true. Those who had not made provision for a long stay had to be supported by those who had.

As things dragged on, I got together with another captain to see if we could arrange a passage home. We took ourselves off for a quiet walk around town, visiting the various airline offices. We were received with every courtesy and cups of tea even, but the various carriers had been warned off and declined to do business with us, One carrier offered some hope, as they had a chartered freighter due to arrive carrying motor cars and, perforce, returning to Italy empty. It might be available for charter. On further enquiry we found this was not so, and the local manager was regretful. We returned to the hotel and reported our lack of progress to the chaps at our now regular chat shows prior to the happy hour. I was hopeful of Mr Cohen of El Al, although he too had shaken his head regretfully. Sure enough, he telephoned the next day. 'I think there is a way we can do business, Captain', he said. I went to his office. Mr Cohen had established the numbers involved including the chaps at Entebbe and multiplied this by the cost of the airfare to London and arrived at what he called a nice little sum. We ironed out any possible difficulties. Money in advance was the chief of these. I mentioned the Kenyan Airline pilots, I felt sure they would underwrite the amount. 'Yes, yes', said Mr Cohen, 'I'm sure they would, if they have that kind of money. I wonder where they bank?' He made a few telephone calls and smiled at me. Apparently they had that kind of money.

When the transports arrived, we made our way to the airport and boarded a flight for Tel Aviv. On the following day we took their regular flight to London. When we arrived at the central area in Heathrow, the word was out that the strike was settled and all was forgiven. I decided to put it to the test. I went to our regular reporting centre to check in and request transport to the car park. The girl refused straight away. 'I believe the strike is over', I said, 'please refer my request to your superiors'. Transport, they replied, was on its way. The strike was indeed over.

When I next went through Nairobi the station manager took me aside. He was disappointed in me, I should have tipped him off before we left. He'd felt rather foolish when he found we'd gone. Straight away I made things worse. 'You might have told the Company', I said, 'and they would have put the mockers on it'. He looked hurt. Back in my home village, the landlord of the Stag and Hounds buttonholed me. 'You chaps', he said, 'you've driven a coach and horses through the government's income policies'. Not quite, perhaps, as there were further hiccups, but we had broken out of the straitjacket. That such actions were ever necessary is a sad commentary on the way we, both pilots and management, conducted our affairs. Probably for the first time in its history, the Corporation was making money, really making money, not just juggling the accounts and talking of operating profits or reducing deficits. In the two previous years they had declared a net surplus of nearly £24 million for 1967 and in 1968 confirmed a profit of £21 million. So, perhaps if it had to be done the hard way, this was a propitious time to choose.

When the hijackings began, no one took much notice. It was mostly confined to the USA and carried out by Cubans. A localised phenomenon. In Britain we are quite used to taking things with a pinch of salt where 'the Americans' are concerned. British newspapers often carry a column entitled, 'This is America', or something similar. All the most outrageous things that have recently happened in the USA are gathered there. Every variation of the 'man bites dog' story, in fact. So even those who should know better are sometimes deceived by this attitude. The hijacking spread to criminals hoping for gain, and then to political activists, and quickly grew to menacing proportions. It spread beyond the shores of the USA and centred upon the Arabs. The nations of the western world were caught out and undecided as to how to combat this menace. The airlines were unable to help, being even more undecided. I can't claim to know any more than the next man, but I did feel strongly that we should oppose the skyjackers, if need be by open defiance, whatever the risk. I found myself alone in these views and so, fell silent.

Now events moved nearer home and the VC10s became a favoured target for the hijackers. The first chap I knew who was thus involved came near to being destroyed by it. When it was all over and the trainers had checked him out again, he himself packed it in and retired. The others I knew, taken over perhaps, in less gruelling circumstances, survived to fly again another day with no apparent ill effect. The airline managers remained as silent on the subject. The security business grew apace, concentrating on passenger search as the first line of defence.

From time to time I would raise the subject with my crew, confining discussions to the technical staff. I soon learnt that if the cabin crew were involved and I ventured an opinion based on defiance and resistance, they became alarmed. Confidence in their captain melted like snow in the sunshine. So I remained uncertain, as uncertain as everyone else, as to what I would do if the worst happened and a hijacker appeared.

And then, one morning my hijacker did appear at Dubai airport. He was a Yemeni and came from Aden and was perhaps the world's most hopeless terrorist. The gun he carried was real enough, as were the bullets. The first I knew of his presence was when a very excited police inspector arrived at the aeroplane. He took me aside, shaking visibly. 'I've just grabbed a gunman', he said, 'one of your passengers, and I've got him under arrest. Here's the gun'. He showed me an ugly looking pistol. 'How did you spot him?' I wanted to know. He had made himself conspicuous, it seemed, by checking in with a suitcase and then, apparently changing his mind, deciding not to travel and demanding that his case be returned. That wasn't possible. His behaviour attracted attention and the police were called. My friend happened to be there on other business and seized him. It was hardly surprising that he was trembling. All this took only a moment to tell. He then asked me where we had come from. I told him, Bombay. 'That's it', he said, 'we could still be in trouble, they get on at different stages, then when they're all together, they make their move. I'll have to have that suitcase off', I said, 'that means everything off and I'll flush them out if there are any more'. I instructed the Inspector to stand beside me in the doorway hidden from sight, with his revolver at the ready. 'You see one come towards me, don't forget, shoot to kill', I told him.

I picked up the public address mike. I stood in the aisle in full view and spoke into it. I told them we had a security risk, an attempted hijack, told them I wanted everyone off and the baggage. When I had everything checked out, then we'd go, not till then. No one moved. I put the mike back on its cradle. The policeman looked a little sheepish. 'It's OK', I said. 'Do one more thing for me; call your opposite number in Bahrain. When I get there I'd like to see the tarmac crawling with police. It'll take about two hours to get this show on the road from now'. I thanked him warmly. Next time through, I enquired about the Yemeni. They had deported him.

On the way back to London, I made out my voyage report. I made it brief. What can you say about a non-event, a non-hijack? The response was even more brief. I didn't even get a reply. When it was over, I asked my first officer what he thought about hijacking now. He looked at me thoughtfully before replying. 'If I could have got my hands on him, if I'd had a gun, I could have killed that bugger', he said.

Plans were going ahead for the next generation of jet aeroplanes. The Boeing Aeroplane Company, now well established as front runner among the aircraft manufacturers, were taking orders for their new widebodied aeroplane, the B747. On the previous time round, when they produced the B707, Pan American's president, the redoubtable Juan Trippe, had been the first to place an order. (He hedged his bets, as it happened, by ordering a similar number of DC8s from the Douglas Aeroplane company). Airline chiefs throughout the western world fell over each other to get in the queue behind him. History repeated itself with the B747. Douglas and Lockheed were right alongside with their widebodied type. When Pan Am ordered the 747, BOAC hastened to join in.

The British and the French were also cutting metal for their supersonic aeroplane, the Concorde. The airlines dragged their feet on this one. In Derby, the Rolls-Royce company had stolen a march on the world with their development of a new material called carbon fibre. They planned to use this new material in their RB211 series of engines, which would be suitable for the new larger transports and rival those of the North American manufacturers. As part of the development work, some VC10 engines were fitted with compressor blades made of the new material and sent down the routes for evaluation.

I had the ill fortune to be operating down to West Africa with one of these engines fitted and I knew no more about it than the brief details given in the maintenance log. As we approached Lagos, a king-sized cumulonimbus cloud barred the way, bringing heavy rain and severe conditions to the area. I decided that discretion was the better part of valour and turned back, diverting to Kano. While we refuelled in Kano, anticipating that conditions in Lagos would improve, I was uneasily aware that, by the time I got there, the next storm might well have arrived and I would be faced with the same problem. Sure enough, that is more or less what happened. The next storm, however, was not as severe as its predecessor and I decided to give it a go. It was fairly turbulent on the descent and we bashed our way through some nasty little cells in heavy rain and thick cloud. The approach procedures at Lagos were very primitive, only a VOR radio beacon with distance measuring equipment and a non-directional beacon that was rendered unreliable by the weather conditions. It was adequate for a cloud break procedure when the terrain is as flat as a pancake, so I pressed on. As we got down towards limits, I liked it less and less. Along with the clearance to land, the tower were warning of heavy rain and standing water on the runway. I decided to chuck it and give Lagos a miss. I opened up the taps to overshoot. The engines responded and we climbed away back into the murk. I called for another diversion, this time to Accra, in the belief that we might be better placed for another attempt there, and besides, Kano had enough of us. The engineer called my attention to one of engines which was showing heavy vibration. It was our friend with the carbon fibre blades. I ordered it shut down. Definitely Accra, we stood a better chance of engineering assistance there.

At some point, when we'd struggled our way through customs, and got through the worst of the hassle that always attended diversions, and managed to avoid any direct confrontation with irate passengers, one of the ground engineers called me over. 'Would you like to see your engine, Skipper?' he asked. 'I've never seen anything like it!' He took me back out to the tarmac and I climbed up the trestles to peer inside the engine. The compressor blades hung in shreds and tatters. 'That's the new carbon fibre', I said, 'you'll have to pull the engine and send it back to Rolls. I'm sure they'll be interested'.

'If that's the new material, Skipper, better sell your Rolls-Royce shares', he advised.

I was rash enough to pass on his advice back in the Kremlin when I made my voyage report. Plainly, the new material didn't like getting wet. By then, plans were far advanced and, in the rethinking and redesigning of the engine, Rolls-Royce went bust. With so much of the economy and the defence effort dependent on Rolls and their products, the government hastened to their rescue. It was ironic that the ruling party at the time was the one that professed not to support nationalisation and lame ducks.

A Super VC10, G-ASGC, of BOAC (Mick Taylor)

In the land of the blind

There were times when the aircrew families, particularly wives, had a pretty bad time of it. The roster ruled our lives. There was no leeway in its inexorable demands, for personal problems or emergencies.

When my father died suddenly, my wife telephoned the Corporation to ask them to tell me and, if possible, to arrange for my return. When I did return ten days later, it was clear to her that they had neither informed me, nor made any attempt to secure an earlier return. Years later, when my second son contracted meningitis and lay close to death, she telephoned again to plead for my return, with exactly the same result.

She made no other demands but went about the business of raising our family and dealing with our household affairs as best she could during my frequent absences. All the aircrew wives did likewise. The toughest part for most of them was the terrible feeling of isolation, the feeling that they didn't exist as far as the Corporation was concerned, It's very different where the husband is home every night, or at least within reach. There was also the fear, unacknowledged, or rarely admitted, that he might not return at all. The news of an aircraft accident in some remote part of the world, could bring a moment of panic and anxiety. After many years and prolonged agitation, the Corporation found its way clear to provide a telephone service whereby wives could ask for return dates and times and have some idea of their husband's whereabouts. Eventually, when the thing got working, the next of kin were advised of delays and re-rostering. My wife enjoys telling the story of the occasion when she was telephoned to be told that her husband was delayed and would be late returning. 'Shall I tell him', she asked, 'or will you, he's just walked in the door!'

To make things harder to bear, neighbours and friends were liable to see only the brighter aspects of the job, the time at home when they were at work, the recurring 'second honeymoons' and the cheap travel to exotic places that they could not afford to visit. They rarely mentioned the drawbacks. One day, back in the Stratocruiser days, returning from a trip, the captain offered me a lift home. As it lay on his route, I gladly accepted. Outside hut Number 221 on the north side at Heathrow, I put my bag in the boot of his car and settled myself on the rear seat while he took the wheel with his wife beside him. We made polite conversation as we drove along, but by the time we had passed the Peggy Bedford public house on the old Colnbrook bypass, the conversation had taken a different turn.

The captain's wife was dying to tell him every detail of his household cares and problems from the moment of his departure and would not be gainsaid. She launched herself on a catalogue of woes and difficulties. He took it badly, conscious of my presence on the back seat but mainly because he was tired and discouraged. By the time we had traversed the dangerously suicidal three lane bit of the bypass, I could see a full-scale row was brewing. Yet both were behaving most naturally and reasonably; the wife anxious to lay down the burden of responsibility and, even earn a word of praise or thanks, and the captain reluctant to shoulder these new problems about which he felt so helpless and, somehow, guilty.

As we came to the traffic lights, I had to shout that anywhere around here would do. It took a while before we came to a stop. 'Yes, yes', I said, 'this will do nicely, yes, I'm sure'. When I got out I left the rear door open. 'The boot', I said, 'my suitcase is in your boot'. We got it sorted out and they drove off down the Great West Road. I walked back towards my house, the suitcase heavy with dirty laundry and reflected on this typical enactment of the aircrew returning home.

It was many years before we met my fellow pilots and their wives in any great numbers. Eventually my wife commented on just how many of the wives seemed to be very assertive, or aggressive even, and wondered aloud if they had developed in that way because of their long experience in the single parent family business, long before the expression gained currency. Or had they always been like that? I was unable to answer but gave thanks that she, at least, had not so developed.

It isn't always easy to keep passengers happy. Nobody likes diversions and delays and both can be expected to generate complaints. On any diversion due to weather you can expect abuse. Some of your passengers are bound to assume that you have some ulterior motive for the diversion. Either you're not up to it; not skilful or brave enough, or you have secret personal reasons for preferring, say Prestwick or Manchester, to London. It's a common experience to find that, barely have you landed and decided to bring the passengers ashore, that the story that the fog has cleared circulates like wildfire. The cry goes up that another carrier, Pan Am or Air France has just landed at your erstwhile destination, or so-and-so have a flight leaving within the next few minutes and seats are available. Where this information comes from no one ever knows. It is not possible to keep passengers informed, once they have got outside the range of the aircraft's public address. You can expect several carping letters of complaint to reach the Company within the next few weeks. Even if it turns out that London is 'socked in' with fog for a week and the media have run the story front page all that time, you will get a letter or two to say that the passengers were not kept informed.

Usually the Company's public relations office managed to deal with these complaints but, just occasionally, a writer was so outraged or the complaint so outrageous that it was considered too hot to handle and got fed back to the captain with a request for his comments. I don't suppose my replies were ever allowed back to the passenger. I had to divert from London on my very first trip in command. After a fairly long flight from New York, finding London below landing limits in fog, I made an early decision and rerouted to Prestwick. When I'd refuelled and after some thought, I decided to cancel the flight and terminate in Prestwick. The station staff got busy arranging passage by train to London. British Rail were always very good, putting on extra coaches, or entire trains if required, when the airlines were grounded by fog. On this occasion, the arrangements got complicated. Another of our aeroplanes had also diverted and followed me to Prestwick. The captain, however, took a different view, and decided that there was every chance of the fog clearing sufficiently for a landing at London. So while I headed for the Railway Hotel he refuelled and waited for his chance at Prestwick. For once, the rumour flashing round that so-and-so had a flight leaving for London, was correct and the bulk of my ex-passengers clamoured to join it.

While I slept the day away, they circled London and, when I got up that afternoon for tea, they were arriving back at Prestwick. I looked up from the teacups and thought I recognised some of the weary, crumpled people checking in, and could hardly resist walking over to make enquiry as to their welfare. The captain decided on another hotel for the night. It could, just as easily have turned out the other way round. On this occasion, however, I was able to redirect the outraged letters to my colleague.

Charlie Maloney was my flight engineer on one trip when we had a delay in Tehran. The incoming Comet crew from London had said that number four engine had run down while they were taxiing in. They hadn't tried to relight – hardly seemed worth it – and they hadn't entered it up in the book. When we were ready to fire up, we tried number four first, with no result. So we let it be, waiting for the starter to cool and got the others turning, returning in between for another attempt at number four. We had no means of knowing this, but number four had seized solid. So we were applying the irresistible force to the immovable object. Down in the electrics bay, the starter panel and its associated wiring gave up the struggle, welded itself solid and caught fire. The aeroplane was plunged into darkness and filled with smoke and the pungent smell of burning rubber. It was time to hit the panic button. The ground crew were quick off the mark, however, and by the time I'd shut down the other three and called for evacuation, the steps had been repositioned and so the aeroplane was evacuated without any great bother. It took some time to establish the cause of our misfortune but it was clear immediately that we weren't going anywhere. Arranging transport and accommodation in the middle of the night at Tehran airport is not something to be undertaken lightly or quickly, but once matters had been set in motion, my crew and I proceeded to the transit lounge to await events. Had there been anywhere else available away from the passengers, I would undoubtedly have chosen it, but there was not.

Presently, Charlie came in with news of the engine and the ruined starter panel and it was clear that we needed another aeroplane if the flight was to continue, and had to arrange for a team of engineers to repair the existing one. I had to get busy concocting more signals for London and ordering more coffee for Charlie. Anyone who has ordered coffee in the transit lounge at Tehran Airport will know that it is not something you forget.

It appeared later, that I might have been better employed in spreading the news among my passengers. Among them was a lady who was very indignant over the delay, even more indignant about the lack of technical data, and moreover, she had lost her shoes, escaped only with her life, and was a friend of the Chairman.

By the time the Chairman sent the letter on to me, I'd put the matter out of my mind, feeling that, with Charlie's help, I hadn't done too badly with a rather awkward situation. The bit in her letter that really hurt was the part about how the crew had done nothing, but sat in the bar ordering drinks. Mischievously, she'd omitted to mention, or to notice, that the drinks were coffee. I doubt very much if the Corporation sent my reply back to the Chairman.

There is such a thing as talking a good operation. Some chaps are better at it than others. Crews and even passengers may say of one chap, what a fine captain he is. Indeed, to be known as a good captain, you have to be fairly good and inspire confidence, and if on top of that you can talk a good operation, your reputation is secure.

I recall having breakfast one morning in the old Imperial Hotel in Tokyo following an overnight flight from Hong Kong. An old decaying typhoon lay along the northern part of the route. Lightning flashed from the embedded storm cells, lighting up the clouds from within in an awesome display. But flying above the system posed no problem until, on our descent into Tokyo, it got turbulent and was fairly vicious from time to time. Behind me I could hear a Qantas flight working and he called me a couple of times. I was able to reassure him that all was well. It would have been nice, I reflected, if I had someone out front to reassure me. I nodded and smiled at a group of my ex-passengers from the night before who came in and sat at the next table. I was tempted to tell them to avoid the fresh orange juice and have the canned. Fresh orange juice in Tokyo is very expensive and you have to be really keen on it to pay the extra. I refrained, as they were British and so was I. Then a whole mob joined us and the dining room filled up. From the conversation, it was clear that they had arrived on the Qantas flight. It was also clear that they had ridden in on the wings of the typhoon and wanted everybody to know about it. I could see my ex-passengers becoming puzzled and curious, wondering when this could have happened. Not last night surely. They too, must have been part of just such an adventure. Maybe I should have told them, maybe I should learn and talk a good operation also. What's the use of riding out a typhoon with nothing more than a jolt or two, if no one knows about it?

It was never my intention to become a training captain. The training manager phoned me one day, quite out of the blue, to ask if I'd be interested in joining what he referred to as his training team. I had to ask for time to think about it. It was certainly going to change my domestic scene and would cut the route flying by half or more. There was no point in lengthy debate: it was yea or nay, so I phoned back to say I'd give it a go. It transpired that I was required in a hurry. I had not been the first choice. My predecessor had undergone the civil aviation authorities course to equip him as a delegated examiner and chucked it. He'd failed the course, I was told. But as it happened, I knew him quite well and immediately went to see him. It was not true that he'd failed the course. He had reservations about the authorities' attitude to conducting tests and, as he would be acting on their behalf in administering instrument rating tests, he would be bound by their rules.

I had a week with one of our simulator instructors, a man well versed in the technicalities of airways procedures and rules of the air. That, and an hour or two in the old Link Trainer refreshed me in the basics. It was just as well. Without it I wouldn't have lasted five minutes at the hands of the examiners at the Civil Aviation Flying Unit at Stansted, near Bishop's Stortford. These were the chaps responsible for administering and conducting all the UK instrument rating tests. In practise, the system worked only by virtue of the appointment of delegated examiners in the airlines to conduct these tests on their behalf. Being the seat of authority and the font of all wisdom in instrument rating matters, they had the reputation of being very tough. I went off to Stansted secure in the knowledge that these things are usually exaggerated and need not be taken too seriously. I was in for a shock. The course was slated to last two weeks. The first two days were devoted to demoralising the candidate and reducing him to pieces. This was quite simply done. The transition from flying large jet transport in a multi-crew situation to the single-handed operation of a small, steam-driven twin, was in itself, something of a handicap. The candidate was asked to fly a full instrument rating on the first day and again on the second. His performance was then subjected to ruthless and destructive criticism.

I did fairly well on the first day, better than I had expected and, although surprised by the detailed and often vicious criticism, felt fairly well content. I determined to do better on the next. It was not to be. I fell into a trap. I accepted a flight level with my air traffic control clearance that the aeroplane could not reach by the point specified. By the time I realised this it was too late. I would reach the reporting point at the wrong level. The examiner intervened to re-clear with air traffic control and I went on to compound the error. The hardest thing you ever have to do in a flying test, if you have made an error, is to continue as if nothing had happened and set the failure behind you. If you dwell on your mistake instead of bringing all your concentration to bear on what you are doing and scanning ahead, you invite further errors and worse, a deterioration of flying accuracy. It happens in real life also, not just in tests, only it's more obvious in a test. So I wound up with several major fail points against me, feeling that I was indeed a bum. The examiners were quick to take advantage.

Any major failure, such as the departure from a cleared flight level or, as in my case, to achieve a specified level, was, in itself, sufficient cause to fail the test. Such failures were thought of as stone hard, or stone-hard certainties and, in the jargon of the unit, were referred to as stone bonkers. This appeared to be derived from 'stone hard' failures, or 'bankers', leading to 'stone bankers' and hence 'stone bonkers'. Stone bonkers needed to be reinforced with as many minor failure points as could be mustered. Although in themselves often trivial, these could be used to build a much stronger case. The entire accent and purpose of the place concentrated upon failure.

The principal aim of the training was to sharpen up the would-be examiner's observance of failures, or 'fail points'. He must learn to appreciate when these were most likely to occur and to record them and not to miss any. By the end of a two-hour instrument flying test, whether using a real candidate undergoing a renewal, or a school guinea pig staff pilot, the examiner was expected to have noted every slight departure from the laid-down tolerances. He was then given ten minutes' grace to put together the findings and make a convincing and unassailable case for failure, either in whole or in part.

By the end of the first week it was clear why my predecessor had rejected the job. There was only one other candidate there, a week ahead of me. He was bogged down in difficulties and immensely depressed. I endeavoured to cheer him up and to divert him from his preoccupations but to no avail. As far as I could find out his difficulties centred around the pre-flight briefings. Great stress was laid upon briefings. Their duration was timed by stop watch. The content had to cover a prescribed list of manoeuvres, every detail of the route to be followed and what amounted to a thinly disguised catalogue of points on which it was possible to fail. The object of this, it was said, was to reassure the candidate, to put him at his ease. In reality, of course, it was to ensnare him in the event of failure, with the comment, 'I did tell you at the briefing to do and so', or worse, 'You did specify 180 knots for the cruise but you flew at 169 knots instead'.

At every attempt my friend was more severely criticised and given yet another list of helpful suggestions and daily became further bogged down. He spent his evenings locked away in his room at the Old George Hotel, frantically repeating his briefings into the microphone of a portable tape recorder or listening to the playback in growing self-criticism and despair. The walls of the Old George bedrooms were thin and eventually I could stand no more. I beat upon his door to tell him that valuable drinking time was being lost and prevailed upon him to save the batteries further punishment and come and recharge his own. But all to no avail. His eyes darted about, unseeing, among the quite unremarkable customers around the bar and the atmosphere of normality and complete, even stupefying, ordinariness, failed to get through to him. When I went to sleep that night I could hear him hammering away. He stuck it out to the end of the week when they put him out of his agony and told him he had been unsuccessful.

I struggled through the two weeks, comforted only by the knowledge that the real world lay just outside and that the ideas and standards of the civil aviation unit could not survive much beyond their corner of Stansted airfield. I admit that there had to be rules to protect both examinee and examiner. I could not, even when invited, hope to devise better rules, especially in the time available. It was only their insistence that the examiner could not exercise any discretion or interpret the rules that made the whole thing unworkable. If rigidly applied, as the Civil Aviation Flying Unit insisted, every commercial pilot in the UK would have run out of instrument rating qualification before the year was out. As the training manager had said, when I protested that I was unsuitable for the job and lacked deep technical knowledge, it was the land of the blind and the one-eyed must lead. A blind eye had to be turned, at times. I had entered the world of nitpickers.

I settled in quickly with the training team. There was a lot to do. At the time, a tremendous number of new pilots were being recruited and trained in almost every flying school in the UK. The airways corporations had combined to sponsor the College of Air Training at Hamble and, when that was filled, places were taken at Oxford and Carlisle and even in far-off Perth. I couldn't foresee a need for so many would-be civil pilots in Britain and went so far as to query the numbers and the urgency of such a massive programme. I think this earned me some pitying looks.[1] It was evident to everyone that when the wartime breed of airmen retired they would have to be replaced over a short space of time. Even if the aeroplanes continued to get bigger and crews smaller, the numbers needed would continue growing. When we had finished the first winter's training season at Shannon, I was struck by the number of landings carried out there that the Irish authorities billed us for. I recall it because, as the last man to leave, I had to bring back the paperwork to London. It exceeded ten thousand landings.

When I left BOAC to go to the Gulf, my friend, Jack, arranged a little lunch party in the Senior Mess. He wanted me to meet one of the senior executives of the company I would be joining. Jack was a Freemason and could arrange such things. When

1 Ten years later, British Airways, the successor to BOAC and BEA, was declaring massive redundancies among their pilot force. In the spring of 1982, only twelve years later, following the retirement of the wartime generation of pilots and voluntary redundancy programmes costing millions in severance payments, over two hundred redundant pilots were still on the payroll (*Daily Telegraph* 4 June 1982).

the senior executive joined us and introductions had been effected, I explained that my new employers had asked me to join them as a training captain. This led to a difficulty. The senior executive had no idea what a training captain did or why it was necessary to have such a chap. The flying side of the airline business was a complete mystery to him. This is not unusual in British aviation circles. The top executives are generally woefully ignorant of what fliers consider to be the essential side of the business. As this state of affairs is common, it is put about that such knowledge is unnecessary: the ability to manage is the important thing. Upon this widely held and generally accepted belief, many businesses and indeed, whole industries have, no doubt, foundered. So to rectify this ignorance, perhaps I'd best explain what the training officer attempts to do.

The training of fliers doesn't stop when they qualify and are licensed. Rather, that's when it begins. A system of six-monthly competency checks, annual instrument ratings and annual line checks, survival and emergency procedure exams, licence medicals and recent experience requirements govern their lives. The tendency is to increase the duration and complexity of these tests. New requirements are added and no one takes away or eliminates the old and outdated ones.

The pilots themselves don't seem unhappy with this regime. Indeed, many seem to derive a masochistic satisfaction from the process. And so, a large and expensive system of administering these checks has come into being, with the airline compelled to provide the checkers and trainers and pay them extra for it. The regulating authorities, by adopting a system of delegated examiners, have shifted the burden of cost to the airline, while keeping some control of the system. The fact that it is the same small group in each airline that fail the tests and have to retake them is scarcely a subject for comment. If you fail a competency check all that happens is that you have to retake it, in whole or in part. You may keep up this pattern over your whole career. You might get lucky and meet a trainer who has both the knowledge and the skill to help you overcome the defect, whatever it is. At worst, and in rare cases, things get so bad that the company will dismiss you as incompetent. Almost invariably, you will get a job with another airline and continue happily. Strangely, you may break out of the sequence if that happens, either because you yourself make a greater effort and it genuinely improves your performance, or the standards set in the competency checks by your new employer are less demanding, or perhaps, more humanely applied.

So the training captain examines his fellow pilots in the various mandatory tests. Upon conversion to a new aircraft type the trainers, when they themselves have converted, train the others. When new pilots are hired, the trainers assess them. In BOAC at the time, large numbers of young pilots were being trained from scratch by the flying schools. When that was completed they came to the airline for further intensive simulator and aircraft training by the training captains. Once they had reached the standard, they were released for line training and route experience, and the element of training at base was gradually tapered off.

When the opportunity for command arises, that is, promotion from co-pilot to captain, the refresher training falls to the training captains and here, because of the importance of this event both to the candidate and the travelling public, careful screening and assessment are required. Then various chores; such as flight testing aeroplanes for their certificate of airworthiness, sitting on selection boards, and committees for this and that have to be shared out. And, of course, to have any validity at all, the training captain has to operate on the routes between times and must maintain his own proficiency and recent experience.

The VC10 was a very fine aircraft in its day. However the two simulators were quite dreadful. Most of a training captain's work is done in the simulator, mostly recurrent competency checks and instrument ratings. I quickly found that there was no way in which they could be improved. Between them lay a great array of cabinets occupying a large room with thousands of thermionic valves glowing red. Each circuit board with its valves had some part to play in the operation of the machine and the possibility of malfunction was enormous.

The training captains had to make assessments against this background. When a company receives authority to carry out check 'flights' on a simulator, as opposed to the real thing, it is held that the equipment is fit for the task, having been tested and approved by the regulating bodies. It then follows that the training captain is not permitted to take into account the shortcomings of the machine, only the shortcomings of the candidate. Despite these limitations, the simulator was an excellent training tool but on many occasions, it wasn't really fit for examination purposes. The best description I ever heard of the simulator's performance came from a line pilot. 'Jeff', he said, 'it behaves as if there was a large steel ball loose inside it and this terrible ball rolls about every time you move the controls'. Since its flying characteristics didn't resemble that of the aeroplane and varied in a random and erratic manner, it struck me that some improvement would be achieved if we gave extra simulator training time. The candidates would then be in 'simulator flying' practice and thus be able to put up a much better performance during the test itself.

I was given the task of rewriting the simulator exercises. Straight away I wrote a two-day routine. The first day was a refresher and the check itself fell on the next day. When I had the complete routine done, I conducted trials with other training captains, and then volunteer line pilots, modifying the programme as we went. When all was complete, I got the Ministry flight inspectors down to observe the system in action and got their approval. My improvements worked like a charm. The check failure rate dropped dramatically. I had the programme copied and circulated to the line pilots so that they could arrive knowing the 'location' of the tests and mug up on all the emergency procedures and equipment failures.

The pilots grumbled about the extra days, but once they realised how much better it was, they gave it their full support. There was some back-biting among my fellow trainers, perhaps because they hadn't thought of it or couldn't admit that there was a problem there, but most of all because Johnny-come-latelies are not expected to make changes. The object of the exercise was to start the move away from checking to the more positive one of training, and here we had made a good start, even dragging the Ministry along with us.

I was surprised by the meagre training I myself had received upon appointment to the training team. Nothing was laid down by way of a syllabus. The only formal training had been the two weeks at Stansted to qualify as a delegated examiner. When the Ministry's flight, operations inspector had seen me conduct a couple of tests, that part was completed.

At Shannon, on the aeroplane, I had to run through a whole range of circuits and landings from the right-hand seat and observed a high level exercise being carried out. After that it was 'do whatever you like, old boy'. I drew up a little programme of things to do and things to observe. One incident won me great kudos at the time. I invited myself along for a night flying detail of circuits and bumps. There were three cadets along with the training captain and the flight engineer. The first chap started out well and, after his stint, the next cadet moved in and off around the field we went again. This chap was having great difficulty with the approach to land, barely getting the aeroplane in the slot before touch down and, as time progressed, he regressed. The instructor sat there offering little but criticism. Eventually, I could stand no more and asked if I might take over to get the hang of it. It was plain as a pikestaff that the cadet was unable to cope with the standard circuit. This involved commencing the descent from fifteen hundred feet on the base leg prior to turning in for a final approach. But turning at precisely the right point to align with the runway, while adjusting the rate of descent to maintain the glide slope, and keeping the speed exactly right, were too much for him. He had lost confidence in himself and in his judgement. As we flew downwind, I took the controls from him and chatted a little about what we were going to do. In fact the remedy was simple. I extended the circuit downwind so that, when he turned in for final approach, he had only one thing to do and that was to get lined up and stay that way. Then, when the runway looked just right to start the descent, he could concentrate on that. Now, for the first time on final approach, he was in the slot throughout. His confidence began to return and, after a few more circuits, I shortened it back to standard size. It went without a hitch and, just to make sure, I had him do another. The young man was delighted with himself, the flight engineer was mightily impressed. The instructor said nothing. In the small world of the training unit, I had now acquired a reputation of being able to work wonders.

My earlier RAF training now stood me in good stead as the instructional techniques, once mastered, were still retained. I did hope, however, that this time I would not be given all the problem children. Among the group there were several chaps who were marvellous instructors with a real gift for the work, but certainly not all. Before long I had made it clear that I didn't think much of my training to be training captain. Word of this must have got to the corporation's training manager. He had been thinking along those lines himself and had, in fact, gone further and had approached his opposite numbers in several airlines and, as far as he could discover, no one had devised such a training course. Some time before, however, the British government had set up training boards for various industries and the airline business had not escaped. They had, in fact, produced a glossy booklet on the subject of training captains, although when they got to the bit as to exactly how this could be done, it rather petered out.

I was then given the task of devising an instructors' course. I could have a small team to assist me, which the training manager would chair from time to time and I was to use the language employed by the training board. The latter stipulation seemed curious. He explained it to me. The training course was to be done in-house, as far as possible, using our own resources, going outside only if strictly necessary. It probably wouldn't look like the course described by the board, but at least if the wording was similar, it would get training board approval and hence, they would pay. If we got it right we might even make a profit.

The team I picked were naturally very disgruntled. Here

was the most junior chap in terms of training, being given the prize. I had to tread warily. I also wanted the chap who had given me the week's Link Trainer briefing and he indeed was most anxious to be there, but his boss said no. The boss of the department wanted to choose who would go and his choice would not necessarily fall upon my friend. In my view, he didn't have anyone else who would do, so I hired Tony in as an outside contractor, unpaid of course. As his job was on the simulator working shifts, he could attend in his own time. All this palace politics was new to me, and I was amazed.

The end result was a bit of a hotchpotch, full of jargon and words like 'environmental'. But the working schedules and the detailed syllabi at the back were quite good. I had to call it a New Instructor's Course to avoid any battles with existing instructors, although I had them in mind also, and there were sections for their benefit too.

I think it turned out better in practice than at the presentation which I had to give. That proved something of a fiasco. My particular boss, the VC10 training manager, disagreed with the entire concept and came along unwillingly. Halfway through, he lost his rag when defeated in some debating point, and walked out. This was not exactly the happy, triumphal success I might have wished for.

Perhaps the best part was the week's ground instruction covering the art of report writing and some training in lecture techniques. For this part, I had obtained the services of a marvellous teacher from Richmond College, who had specialised in teaching such techniques to mature students. Although one week was far too short, it was still very good value. I don't know if the Air Training Board stumped up or not but I found out later that at least two foreign airlines had shown an interest in it and wanted details. So I was reasonably content. A poor thing, but mine own, was how I saw it.

The work itself was tiring and demanding and, at times, even dangerous, There is always in training, the danger of going too far in simulating a failure, which at the very instant of failure courts the possibility of a real emergency arising. It is ironic that accidents in training exceed those of the real world, although the immense and recent improvement in simulators may well have reversed the trend. Where simulators can realistically represent the failure, there is no longer any merit in attempting that manoeuvre in a real aeroplane in the real world. At the time of which I write, it was still necessary or perhaps only sometimes customary, to repeat all the simulator training in the real aeroplane.

The greatest demands placed upon both men and machines arose on the command courses that had become the aviation equivalent of a commando assault course, culminating in a sort of round Britain cross-country flight, plagued by failures and problems of every kind. This had become known as the Round Britain Quiz, named after from the BBC radio show. It seemed to me, as a newcomer to this now well-established rigmarole, that things had got badly out of hand and it was hardly surprising that the failure rate was high among the co-pilots whom I, of course, knew well from flying with them around the routes year in and year out. I was careful to keep my opinions to myself, but set about making what minor improvements I could, and to endeavour to change established outlooks and attitudes. The Corporation had just commenced a programme of promotions, anticipating slightly the start of retirements by the existing captains as the postwar bulge retired. Promotions had been slow for both generations, and for the chaps now coming up, the wait had stretched out from ten to twelve and then fourteen years. In this long-enforced wait, men became discouraged and began to go stale.

As someone observed of Anthony Eden awaiting the mantle of leadership from Winston Churchill, 'They have kept him in the right-hand seat too long'. The right-hand seat mentality was difficult to counter where the ability to make and execute decisions had atrophied. The manner in which the command courses were conducted aggravated this, as it had become a once-for-all, never to be repeated opportunity. What should have been a routine matter; a review of the requirements of the captain's job, a familiarisation of flying from the left-hand seat and an opportunity to review failure and emergency procedures had been elevated to a monstrous test of flying skills and recurrent constant examinations. The atmosphere and standards of the check flight had spread to every aspect of the course.

To disturb or alter this consensus outlook was not only difficult but dangerous and led to accusations of that standards were being lowered. 'Standards' or 'the standard' were terms much in use and much abused. Everyone knew what they meant yet none could define them. Certainly, to change anything or make things easier was seen as tantamount to lowering the standards. It was as if, locked away in our aviation-sized briefcases, we carried a set of measures that were stamped and hallmarked, guaranteed not to vary, and could be laid out and set against a man's performance, which was checked and weighed and compared with the master set, then pronounced satisfactory or wanting in some respect. Human beings fit uneasily into any such set of measures. However, there must be some set of values, some standard by which to judge, some level of acceptability. This is not so easily defined. At the end of the day, it seemed to me, the standard we all used was based upon our own ability. If the man came somewhere close to one's own idea of the level of competence needed to perform a particular manoeuvre, or bettered it, then, clearly he had reached the standard! That was as close as I ever came to understanding the business of standards, and I think I may be closer than most if we are to judge by the protests and outrage that became evident if ever the subject came up for discussion.

I began to realise that there were more blanks in my New Instructor's Course than I had first imagined. I was told that I would not be involved with command courses, certainly not in my first year as a trainer. The first year was a probationary period, a trial period for both the Corporation and the newcomer. This seemed reasonable. The winters were the periods of maximum training activity. It was then that aircraft and men could be spared. This was the time when the aircraft noise and pollution had reached a peak of unpopularity in the public mind. Airfields throughout the UK were closed at night, or imposed restrictions of all kinds and training flights were unwelcome everywhere.

It was left to the Irish to provide just the airfield and the facilities required. Their airfield at Shannon, now overflown by most transatlantic flights, welcomed the income from the trainers and they came from all over Europe for circuits and bumps. The air traffic controllers were grand, fitting three or four training flights in to their circuit pattern, adjusting to individual requirements, dispersing them when line traffic appeared and doing it all safely, efficiently and with great good humour.

The transfer from line flying to training brought a considerable change in lifestyle. Line flying involves long absences from home, but it also brings long periods of leisure and a generous amount of spare time, both down the routes and at home. I suddenly found that this had vanished. I had to rearrange the garden layout, disappearing the vegetable garden and several flower beds to reduce the labour content. Hobbies such as messing about with boats and radios and, perhaps most regretted, old motor cars, had to be curtailed. And reading, the most invaluable, indeed lifesaving recreation down the routes, disappeared for a time altogether.

In addition to the weekly programme of training details, there were the odd jobs, which as a new boy I had not learnt to avoid, and indeed I sought them out in order to be cleared and fully qualified. Air tests was one such job. These were not the glamorous air tests associated with test pilots, but run of the mill air tests on a well-proven type forming part of the Certificate of Airworthiness. Airline pilots, in any case, don't make good test pilots, their job has made them inclined to caution, to stay well within the boundaries of the operating envelope. Passengers, as a rule, prefer it that way. Nevertheless, the opportunity to fly the aeroplane with no other purpose than to put it through its paces is not to be missed. In addition to checking that all the systems and equipment function as intended by the manufacturers, performance has to be checked against the published schedule. In so doing, a great degree of accuracy in flying is necessary and, in fact, the one that is put through his paces is the pilot. Air tests were usually called up in midweek. Then there followed a series of delays, as the last of the ground runs or functional checks didn't work out, and a day or two's postponement was not uncommon. You could bank on Sunday morning, generally fairly close to the start of morning service. You could count on a good turnout as, traditionally, the tradesmen who had been working on the overhaul were expected to show confidence in their handiwork by being aboard for the air test. Then the observers, with their stopwatches and clipboards had to be there, along with others not readily identifiable. Traditionally also, Sunday morning working brought its own rewards by way of double time payments.

I remember particularly, one air test on a Sunday morning, blessed with perfect late summer weather. We threaded our way among the parked aircraft around the hangars to the nearby threshold of runway 28R. I had filed for, and accepted, a clearance to the south-west between the airways, which left a narrow gusset of clear airspace over the West Country. The climb segments and the high altitude parts of the test went well, moving smoothly from one section to the next with a minimum of delay in setting up the configuration and change of requirements. The next part was to reduce altitude from the performance ceiling to the denser stuff below for the stall tests. The quickest way down is the emergency descent with full air brakes and maximum speed. We set ourselves up for the pressurisation to fail and, as the klaxons started their persistent alarm, banked steeply into the descent as the rubber jungle of oxygen masks appeared in the cabin. Below twenty thousand feet I eased out and we tidied up for the next section, the approach to the stall.

When you design an aeroplane with the engines at the rear, you obtain several advantages and one quite serious disadvantage. You have to mount the tailplane and its control surfaces well away from the engines. This gives the familiar high tailplane or T tail. If this type of aeroplane gets into a stall it is unlikely to recover. The tailplane gets into the turbulent wash of air from the stalled wings and, blanketed in this way, the control surfaces are useless. The condition is known as a deep stall. The designer arranges that, before the aeroplane approaches the stall, a battery of warnings is set off. The most important is the stick shaker or knocker. In case that too be ignored, a stick pusher is fitted. This device is designed to fire off before the aeroplane is truly stalled and, by pushing the stick hard forward, the stick shaker recovery is set in train. Someone has to check that these devices will operate if needed and the Certificate of Airworthiness air test provides such an opportunity. So, with due regard for safety, that is, with someone set to watch the incidence meters especially fitted for the occasion, and another to cross-check the minimum safe airspeed, I made a start.

To reach this stalled condition requires a fair amount of determination and even physical strength. As the speed bled off and the whole aeroplane began to shudder, joined by the stick shakers coming on song, I waited, maintaining the heavy back pressure on the control column. As the airspeed continued to fall, I became aware that the starboard wing was dropping and I was wrapping in control to keep the wings level. Sensing that I was about to run out of control, I released the back pressure and started the recovery. As the ailerons became effective again I had to unwind rapidly to stay level. I completed the recovery. My crew were heads down busy with their figures. I ventured a comment on the rather nasty wing drop. No one had noticed anything untoward. I had to repeat the whole process, partly to show them and to note the control displacement needed to keep the wings level, but partly to ensure that I hadn't somehow screwed it up first time round. There was no doubt about it: the aeroplane had developed a marked wing drop as it came to the stalled condition, instead of its normal straight ahead, wings level characteristic. I spent a little while just flying around clearing the space below me, and setting up for the next section. I slowed the aeroplane and set the flaps and slats for the repeat with everything hanging. There was no problem. Everything functioned as intended, no wing drop, only the stick push was two, maybe, three, knots late. A bit nerve-racking, that: how long do you hang in there? But otherwise it was as sweet as a nut. I cleaned up again and proceeded with the test. There was a lot of minor stuff to come that didn't need my full attention.

I thought about the stalls and the wing drop. There was a clue there somewhere, and I couldn't think it out. My co-pilot suggested a clearance to base, we could dovetail the remaining checks with the return. The ground engineers took it badly. All was set for a quick signing of certificates and the best part of the day remained. Only nineteen defects, all minor, had been logged, but what the hell was the skipper on about? They crowded round to listen. I couldn't sign the Certificate of Airworthiness. That was flat. We had moved into uncharted territory. What were they to do — how could they overcome the snag? I said I'd have to think about it, and asked them just to hang about, and top up the fuel as before. I might have to fly it through again.

I went ashore. I knew one of the other guys who'd had a problem on his last Certificate of Airworthiness test so I phoned him. It was Sunday lunchtime and he was distinctly unhelpful. Whatever his problem had been, it wasn't the same. I didn't want to hear it. I recalled the words of the pilot from the Air Registration Board (ARB) who had cleared me for these flights. 'Don't forget', he had said, 'if you need help, that's what we're here for'. I needed help.

His wife answered the phone. He was out, or not available. Probably in the pub, I thought, Sunday lunchtime, sensible chap. Did she have the number of his deputy, I asked? She did. He was sweeping up leaves in the garden. He wasted no time in covering the distance between Redhill and London Airport. By the time he arrived we were fuelled up and ready to go. I'd made another, minute inspection of the aeroplane, especially the wing leading edges and the slats and their seals. I couldn't fault them. He was a very bright young man. You didn't have to use words twice. Word had gone out that the skipper had brought in the ARB. Confidence had been restored.

We headed back over south-west England in brilliant sunshine. He took it towards the stall a little more rapidly than I had done, a little quicker than my cautious one knot per second rate of decay. He ran into the wing drop just as I had done. I watched him wrapping in control and unwrapping it even faster during the recovery. I felt fairly smug. Speaking rather slowly he said he'd like to do that again, with my permission, and would I follow him through and push, if at any time I didn't like it. He set it up again. I think we both got a little nervous and pushed together. The recovery was more dramatic than intended.

I got a clearance back to London and turned to intercept the airway Green One as instructed. We chatted quietly between times. We agreed that we'd come close to getting into a spin that last time. I wondered aloud how long it was since I'd practised spin recovery. After a bit, the ARB pilot remarked, 'I think I've got it'. We had to wait until after we'd landed as things got busy and we'd threaded our way to the hangars and got on chocks.

The bright young pilot looked at me. The flight deck was crowded with expectant faces. 'It's the wing fences', he said, and paused for dramatic effect.

'The wing fences?' I repeated. 'Of course, the outer wing fence. Just remind me what they do?'

He explained what the fences did. They helped direct the airflow straight back over the wing and stopped the outward span-wise flow at the wingtips. Without them the wingtips would stall before the rest of the wing. I resisted the temptation to poke my head through the DV window to see if the starboard fence was still there. He went on to say that the standard VC10 had wing fences extended right to the leading edge. That being so, there was a fixed fence on the wing and a moving part attached to the slats that formed the leading edge. Between them there had to be a seal, not visible from the ground. By now we were racing ahead of him. The seal must be missing or damaged. The small jet of air finding its way through the gap, he continued, must be sufficient to give early onset of the stall at the right-hand wing tip, with consequent loss of lift and, hence, the sharp wing drop. It was masterly. By the time we had disembarked, there were trestles in place and cries that the fence itself was bent and the seal damaged. Solemnly, we climbed the trestles and inspected the seals. All was revealed. We were accorded every civility and due respect at the certificate signing. I thanked the bright young man most warmly for his help. He headed off on his tortuous journey south from Heathrow, back to Surrey and his overdue lunch.

I made it to the right turn off the motorway and north on the Farnham road past Slough, feeling pretty good. I fancied that the smoke of bonfires from burning leaves hung in the air along with the exhaust fumes. I was glad that I wasn't a real test pilot, just a run of the mill everyday airline pilot, keeping well away from the edges of the flight envelope. On the Monday, the ARB called up inspections of wing fences on all the fleet. I was interested to learn that several were found to be defective.

Certainly, the hardest work and always the most vital in the training units calendar were the command courses. Getting the crosswind landings done was often a problem when the weather failed to oblige. We had to recourse several times to Keflavik where the winds were frequently strong and, with its three runways, one of them had to be out of the wind. Doing one or two crosswind landings within the certificated figures for the aeroplane is one thing, but sitting in on a dozen or more as each man tries his hand and works up to confidence, is quite another.

When the worsening Irish situation had driven us from Shannon and, regardless of expense, we had to recourse to training at Prestwick in Scotland, I awoke early one morning, startled by the rattle of the window in its frame and the buffeting of the wind on the building. I was due to take the early detail so I went to the window, all prospect of sleep gone, and looked out on the slate rooftops of Ayr. As my eyes became accustomed to the slow glimmer of the dawn, I could see that we would have wind aplenty, but from its direction, I would have to use the short runway. I'm not over-fond of crosswinds or of short runways and, in combination, I would rather not do so. I phoned the Met. office.

A cheerful Scottish voice answered. I explained and he assured me that I would have wind all right, but he couldn't oblige with a crosswind, it would only be 20 to 30 degrees off the runway heading, between the west and north-west. 'It's the short runway I'm thinking of,' I said. 'Och aye', he replied, 'that should be interesting'. He made a great sound of the R in interesting. He was right. I had to steel myself a bit to make a start, I could not ask anyone to do something I would not first tackle myself. Only then could I judge whether they were doing well or ill. I took the left seat for a starter, that made me feel better in itself and, being marginally over landing weight, ran the first approach and touchdown on the long runway, into wind. That gave me the feeling of it and the measure of the chop on the approach. It also gave my co-pilot a run at resetting the controls on the touch and go, with plenty of time in hand so that he wouldn't muff it when we got on to the short runway.

All went well, I made a nice touch down on the main runway, 31. We reset the controls and opened up again, and climbed ahead towards Goat Fell. Then a left turn, straight into the downwind position and into the landing drills for the short runway. I made an enormous allowance for the drift as we went downwind and, even then, I could see from the familiar coastline that it was only just enough. I turned on to base leg, knowing that the wind was now behind me, and if I misjudged the turn in, and left it too late, I would never recover the centre line. On that runway you can't afford a wide circuit: the ground to the south is rising rapidly and you can't buy more time that way.

The approach looked good as I turned in, turning through the runway heading to lie in the drift, setting a fairly steep descent with the ground falling away below. It was choppy all right but not too bad; the airspeed bouncing around but holding a nice mean, and I realised for the first time that I was looking through the co-pilot's windscreen, such was the drift on the approach. I realised that I could have made life a good deal easier for myself if I had stayed in the right seat, but there was no time for regrets.

Into the flare, close the throttles, push the body straight to align the runway, wrap in the aileron to hold the left wing down, stop the wind getting under that wing, don't let her drift and we're down just as we've lost the crab. Not quite, the wet surface prevents the bite of rubber on dry concrete. Hold her straight, kill the speed brake, start the flap running, start the trim, pour in the power, ignore the take-off warning horn. 'V1 and rotate', and we're off again. Level off at twelve hundred feet and climb out of the seat for the first of the musical chairs. 'Let's have the first man for shaving'. We settle down to work. Nasty, difficult, dangerous work. Thank you sweet Jesus for another day.

The two nationalised airways companies came together again over pilot training after purchasing the small airfield at Hamble. Every year, knocking on 2,000 young men looked up from their school desks to answer the call. The permanent selection staff filtered out the most likely lads and devised a two-day selection process to get right down to the 200 or so required to start. Although the selectors were quite capable of completing the process, the two Corporations sought to keep a finger in the pie and sent along a practising aviator or two, to sit on the selection board. I would have been very happy to beg off when they asked me if I'd care to sit in on this, but I did feel that it was an honour to be asked and something of a privilege too.

The candidates had to undergo a battery of tests designed to prevent the fitting of square pegs into round holes. I asked if I might sit them myself, the better to understand the results when these were brought into the final assessments. With the solitary exception of a good pass in mental arithmetic, I failed them miserably. Under the guidance of the full-time selectors, I soon got the hang of it. The candidates came for two days of examinations and interviews. We made them play games in imaginary car rallies and debate all the pop subjects of the day, and then more games with real dominoes. We didn't have the facilities for the more robust armed services games with short planks and empty oil drums and ropes.

At the end of the two days we sat down to reconcile the scores. We had to take it in turn to read our own assessments without the benefit of knowing what the others thought. I consoled myself with the knowledge that it didn't much matter. Of the chaps who came up for the final shuffle, we could have taken the first across the threshold, or any other arbitrary score, with equal success, such was the quality of the young men coming forward. All we did was to skim off those who showed up best on the day.

There were times when I felt it went badly for the country lads, and especially for the Scottish boys. While their Surrey counterparts were driving about in the family car and could claim with some authority to know what went on under the bonnet, the Scots lads of the same age would still be limited to a bicycle, and their fathers, I felt, were unlikely to let them clean the family car, never mind drive it or even look under the bonnet. Dennis was always amused when I put up a plea on their behalf from some belated stirring of nationalism.

When these young men completed their initial training, some of them came to us on the VC10s for the type training and it was always a pleasure to work with them and enjoy their enthusiasm for flying.

I can't say that I ever shared that enthusiasm. It was, of course, *de rigueur* right from the first application to stress the love of flying. So many people have said to me that they love flying that I am forced to believe them. How fortunate they are. I can't say that I ever loved it. A pilot's wife told me that she dreaded the time when her husband had to give up flying. He so loved his flying, she couldn't see how he would manage without it. I knew her husband's flying only too well and, I don't think it was the flying he loved, but the lifestyle that went with it.

For me, flying was only a part of the life that brought its own rewards. There can be few professions that put you at a comparatively early age in charge of a large and expensive machine that makes it possible to traverse the world. To be in command of such a flying machine, able to control and guide it is, in itself, marvellously satisfying. Other men buy themselves fast and expensive motor cars in a poor imitation of that thrill. On every flight you have reached the top of the profession and, for the duration of that flight, you are certainly the key figure. This remains true, even although the captain's role has changed. From the earliest days of the pioneers when they battled through alone, then gradually became exalted figures with a large specialist crew to assist them, the wheel has come full circle, shedding the crew as modern technology has supplanted them, and leaving only the pilot and his first officer up front. The present standard three-man crew will be down to two on the latest airliners now under construction in California. Whatever the numbers, it is immensely gratifying. 'When you disappear off the end of two eight left', one supervisory captain said to me, 'remember to reappear out of the murk on the appointed date and time, and all will be forgiven'.

By 1973 the pressure of work on the training unit had eased. The stream of cadets from Hamble dropped to a trickle and the main bulge of the command courses were through. But the recruiters were still busy bringing in young pilots from the RAF when the fuel crisis struck. When the Arabs first used their oil as a weapon against Israel and the West, the airlines were affected immediately. Finding fuel supplies to keep the commercial services going was given top priority and there was nothing left over for training. We wound up with a group all set for the last stages of training and no means of completing them.

Then, quite by chance, someone discovered that Prestwick was holding large fuel stocks for which there had been little demand from the commercial services. We persuaded the maintenance section that they had an aeroplane to spare and laid on a training detail to Prestwick. It was to be a one-off affair and it went out on a Friday afternoon just as the exodus was beginning from the headquarters building. We took a full team of instructors and spares, including our spare course of pilots. They were delighted when they realised what was afoot, as their prospects, so sadly blighted, had now improved considerably.

From first arrival we pounded the circuit, breaking off only to observe the ban on flying during the Sunday morning church services. Hardly had the ministers said goodbye to their flocks when we were airborne again. On Sunday evening, my immediate boss, the fleet training manager called a council of war. He knew that on Monday morning the telephones would start jangling and he would be called to account. But one more day was all that we needed. Also, unless we could put them off for one more day, all the fuel we had used would be wasted. But, with the extra day, we'd be back for sure on Monday night, course completed. Besides, it would take London twenty-four hours to decide and give a firm recall.

This worked. They gave us another twenty-four hours and, stretching that out, we brought the aeroplane back on the Tuesday, checking out the last man on the flight south. I thought there would be trouble, but no, the officials were secretly quite pleased and my boss's reputation was usefully enhanced. Moreover, we had all enjoyed ourselves immensely.

I had to pause and take stock of where I'd got to. The new widebodied aeroplanes were with us and I was getting stuck with the old. The introduction of Concorde couldn't be far off and, along with every right-minded Brit, I'd have liked to have finished on that. But, as the Concorde continued to be delayed, and I continued to get older, this prospect receded. Once more, you had to be specially selected and, although in time everyone can be specially selected, time was not on my side. I made a bid for the B747 and had an encouraging reply, but was told, 'not yet'. I knew that if I delayed much longer I would run foul of the three-year rule. Unless you could offer three years on the type it was not thought economic to be given the conversion course. It seemed plain that the older and more thirsty aeroplanes would have to give way rapidly to the newer and more economical ones. The higher fuel prices were likely to remain in place, with consequences as yet unseen, but the early demise of the VC10 seemed likely.

Then came news of the amalgamation. The two nationalised airlines, BOAC and BEA were to be amalgamated. After the war some very convincing arguments had been put forward to justify having separate airlines. These arguments were now stood upon their heads to justify their being combined. We were renamed British Airways and a plan to repaint the aeroplanes in new colours was hastily put in train. The BOAC staff started a campaign to save the Speedbird, the company emblem which adorned the aeroplanes and was the R/T call sign. It was reminiscent of the public campaign to save the sixpence, which started when the currency became metric and public feeling, reluctant to accept change, centred upon some trivial aspect and objected. The Speedbird was saved.

In what used to be called the Persian Gulf a consortium of Arab states decided to buy Gulf Aviation from the newly renamed British Airways. This was the last of the associated companies, the feeder airlines that had developed to serve the local community and feed passengers to the BOAC main line routes. There was a romantic legend that Gulf Aviation was the successor to Neville Shute's one-man airline in that wonderful yarn, *No Highway*. Be that as it may, from pottering around the Gulf with a few local services, Gulf Aviation was to move into the big time. As part of the deal, British Airways was to provide a fleet of VC10s at knock down prices and give help to get them into international service between the Gulf states and London. Amidst all the fearful problems posed by this sudden decision, the small staff that went to make up Gulf Aviation set to with a will to achieve the impossible, a start date of 1 April 1974.

Someone realised that they would need a training captain. A desperate call went out, and went unanswered. But when the job was offered to me I decided to take it. This wasn't a rational decision. There I was, sitting pretty in a good position, slogging on towards a maximum pension and honourable retirement, and I was being offered a real bag of nails, sight unseen. BOAC, as I still thought of them, agreed to release me. My family made no objection and my wife, staunch as ever and game for anything, thought it would do us good, get us out of the rut. In that she was dead right. When I decided to leave the old BOAC, now rechristened British Airways, in its enforced and ill-fated merger, two other instructors decided to do the same for quite separate and unconnected reasons.

Jack had been offered a job as a flight inspector in Australia. It had fallen through once but was now reinstated. Russ had simply decided that he could afford to go and wanted out. This left the training section a bit short-handed. I got the impression that I was blamed for this miniature exodus and I came under a cloud. There was a lot to do in rearranging my affairs and my wife was due to go into hospital. That was worrying enough in itself. I could have used some time off to give these matters my attention, but it was not to be.

It was plain from the embarrassment of the training unit's secretary that she was under orders to extract the last ounce from me and roster me for routine training chores right up to the very last minute. This she did. I made no complaint and fitted it all in. It is said that, if you want something done, you should ask a busy man, and so it was with me.

My very last detail was routine night continuation training with three of our young second officers. It was a fine night and I chose Stansted as the venue. We pounded the circuit there for close on three hours, and all the young men did very tidy work with nicely judged approaches and landings. I took the return clearance on the run, taking off towards the airways and levelling below the controlled airspace while calling London centre. I had to be back by eleven o'clock when the airport closed. Without further ado they cleared me into the area, passed me to radar and fed us into the approach procedures. I managed a quick flip back to Stansted to wish them goodnight and good luck and then concentrated on the return. I taxied back through the maze of lights that mark the taxiways and runways of Heathrow, over to the North Pen, and the darkness of the maintenance area. A ground engineer appeared, pushing a set of rickety trestles up to the door. I told the boys they could go; no inquisition tonight, I said, they'd all done very well. They disappeared across the tarmac towards the dark bulk of the multi-storey car park. I remember resisting the temptation to write something in the tech. log along with the defects. Something on the lines of my annual, 'And a Merry Christmas to all our readers'.

Back in the deserted office block I turned on the lights and sat down at our secretary Corinne's, desk, I got out the training files and entered up chapter and verse, happy to be writing up good reports as my swan song. I opened the catering pack, my first opportunity to inspect its contents that evening. I'd best be careful not to get crumbs on her desk. I thought about some coffee. The kettle and the instant powder were there but no milk, so I decided to forego it. For some reason, I glanced at my watch. It was well past midnight.

I realised with a shock that it was all over. They had stopped paying me at midnight. I was into extra time. Carefully and methodically, I put the files away and locked up. The senior management pilots had taken to meeting their colleagues off the last flight. There would be photographs for the company magazine, handshakes and, maybe, even champers. I must have missed them in the darkness of the North Pen. I made my way out of the building to hunt for my car in the multi-storey. That was it, I thought, they'd be waiting there to surprise me. They didn't show. I left as I had come, some twenty-seven years before, unheralded and unsung. I'd have liked to have met the medic who started my file with his prognosis, 'A poor long term risk.' After twenty seven years of blank pages, what could he have added to round it off, I wondered?

Even Mr Hanratty of the uniform section let me down when I managed to get there to hand in the uniform. I took along the old Comet oxygen mask and head gear. I was short of two tie clips. Tie clips didn't count, so I was all complete. I thought he might write down the value of the raincoat, about ten shillings would be right. It was the only thing worth retaining. He made no move, but went on about the suppliers and the impossible task of getting white cotton shirts. I thought that my wife would have liked a word on that one. Ironing those ridiculous, old-fashioned garments was the one thing she wasn't going to miss. I let him have the raincoat. He chucked it on a pile of discarded garments on the floor. Ah well, I thought, its not going to rain much where I'm headed and I'll not be suffering from the cold either, so I let it go.

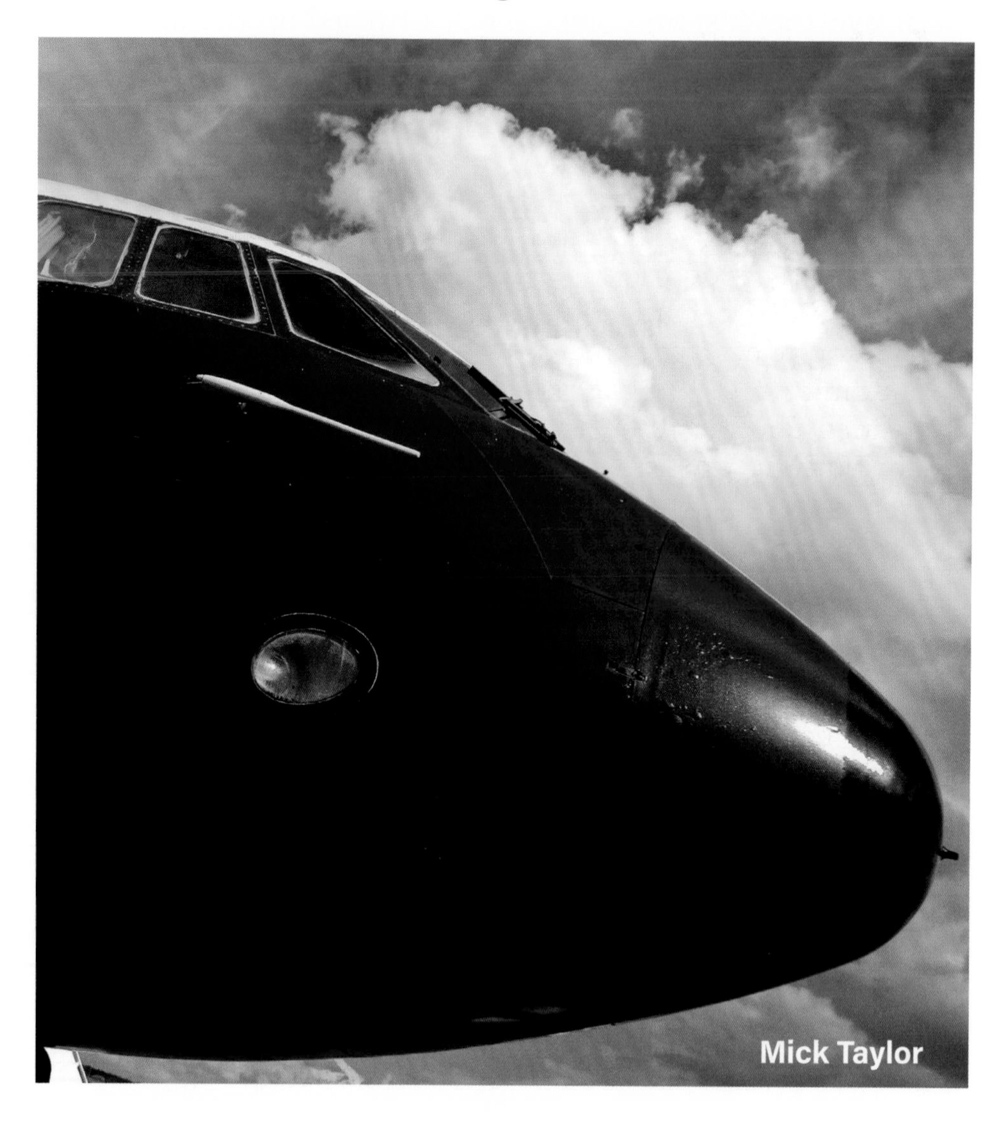
Mick Taylor

The way ahead

After six summers in the Gulf, we both felt we'd had enough. The fun had gone out of the job. I realised that the fault lay with me, not with the flying, so I made my excuses and mentioned family reasons in my formal letter or resignation. My wife and I left Bahrain to make it home for Christmas in 1979, and collect our scattered family together once more. We left without regrets and never a backward glance, and in the knowledge that we had left many good friends behind us.

As the 1980s began, I had one final chore to do for Gulf Air. Two young pilots appeared, scions of important families. They were admitted to the company without question and were to be trained for TriStar just as soon as arrangements could be made. Nothing was known of their training background or of their performance. A potentially difficult situation arose for the company's training pilots. It was resolved by hiring me as an outside contractor, thus giving the company an out, in case they failed to reach an acceptable standard. Happily for me, although they were completely different in outlook and temperament, both were natural pilots. Less happily and, possibly because of their rank and station, we found curious gaps in their knowledge. I thought that their early training must have been military in character, switching later to civilian, and lots of hard work would be needed to fill the gaps.

I had to take them through the simulator training, right up to check out and try for a sound competency check and instrument rating. So I started by taking the syllabus apart and reassembling it in a different order. It had been written for experienced pilots and covered a lot of complicated European routes and airports with standard instrument departures and arrivals. This obscured the aim of the exercises without adding anything worthwhile and, although I appreciated the author's good intentions, it is a sometimes mistake to try to make a simulator behave exactly like an aeroplane. Used for competency checks, you really have to strive for realism, but on conversion training the simulator comes into its own, with stop and freeze, instant reruns of approaches, putting in sixty minutes to every hour.

Treated in this way, the students made rapid progress. In two days they had the lengthy start up drills buttoned up and, by the end of the first week they were pretty solid on hand flying and normal operations. The second week saw them through the more difficult emergency and abnormal operation, and by week three they were able to tackle the automatics and the airways work. At the end of the normal allocation of simulator time, one student was ready for check, but his colleague lagged behind due to weaknesses in his procedural airways work. I arranged to farm him out to an old BOAC friend, Tony Angel, who was a partner in a small simulator business, for a week's cramming on procedures. That did the trick and I gave him a further three sessions to consolidate, and put him up for a check. Like his friend before him, he passed comfortably and I sat in on it just to see how it went.

That night, when I walked across the car park from my last ever simulator detail, and drove off down the motorway, I was well content. Right at the end, I felt that the old magic had not deserted me. The fact that this knowledge was confined only to a privileged few perched in a box of electronic gear balanced on hydraulic stilts, somehow made it more precious, not less. Thus I took my final bow and left the aviation stage.

Epilogue

And of course, there were regrets. Not too many but, as in any walk of life, there were missed opportunities and things I might have changed if I'd had a push-button freeze and instant re-run.

I'm sorry I didn't have the chance to fly the Queen. When my daughter was small, she said to me one day, 'Dad, why don't you ever fly someone good?' That *would* have been good. I'm sorry I didn't have the chance to fly Concorde. That might have been good or it might have been disastrous. You had to be very special indeed to fly Concorde in British Airways and, besides, I'd left too soon. I'd have gone on believing that, if I hadn't heard from friends in Braniff of Texas, that such claims were nonsense. As in the past, British Airways had continued to apply rules of strict seniority. If Concorde couldn't be flown by ordinary senior pilots, there had to be something wrong with the damned aeroplane.

There were also times when I regretted becoming involved with training, seeing it as little more than side issue or an irrelevance. Just because it was interesting, or challenging, doesn't, of itself, make it more valuable than flying the line. There can be no doubt about that flying the line is what it's all about: the only real and worthwhile job in civil aviation. Therefore, a great deal of what I did, or attempted to do, in the darkened simulator rooms, could just have well been done by others, or left undone. If I'd stuck to line flying, as I'd stuck to the main force in Bomber Command, I'd have come out well ahead on flying hours and probably ahead in job satisfaction, and far more certain of the relative value and importance of things in aviation.

That's really not much of a list compared with all the things

I don't regret. An airline job can be pretty dull at times and it's a strange, self-contained little community shut away inside its metal tubes or isolated in hotel rooms trying to sleep when the rest of the world is awake. But the compensations outweigh all this. To be in charge of such marvellous and powerful machines, circumnavigating the world, pitting a mere man's skill and knowledge against the elements, to reappear out of the murk over the threshold of 28 left at the appointed time with nothing bent, nor stood into hazard, gives rise to a feeling of achievement and immense satisfaction.

Over the course of the years a great store of knowledge is accumulated. It's called experience. Much of it is rapidly outdated. An intimate knowledge of the incidence of low cloud and stratus over the airfields of Newfoundland, once so necessary to the North Atlantic operation, has long been irrelevant. The same applies to setting up the Smiths flight director for the hold at Digger's Rest in South Australia. Some things, such as how to backtrack the RAF needles when flying away from the station, and get it right, and not turn the wrong way, remain important as old equipment and techniques linger into the age of high technology, and some things are so beloved of check pilots and examiners that they live on in the check world long after their demise in the real. It seems a pity that so much experience should be wasted. On retirement, there is a tendency to think of becoming a consultant or an advisor to the industry, as happens in other fields. I think this is a snare and a delusion. The pace of development in aviation is now so rapid that a year out of the left-side seat sees the beginning of an ever-widening gap. Unless you are still actively involved in doing the job, what you have to say is no longer valid. The industry is better advised to look forward, not back. But time and hindsight does give perspective, and commenting on past events may be worthwhile and provide guidelines for the future.

I am most concerned for British Airways. I declare an interest: I receive a pension from the British Airways Pension Fund and the corporation is a major contributor to the fund. Their continued existence and financial good health is important to me. However, I also believe it to be important to Britain. I should be sorry to see our major airline take the same route into oblivion as so much of British industry. There is no reason to suppose that private enterprise could do better if British Airways was split up: rather the reverse. Check the record of past performance. There have been a lot of Freddie Lakers in the past.

There can be little argument that the amalgamation of BOAC and BEA was a mistake. Both partners fought it bitterly and continue to do so. Ten years later, the correspondence columns of the pilots' magazine, The *Log*, is devoted, almost exclusively to recriminations between long-haul and short-haul pilots. The few who can get a word in edgewise try to persuade the warring factions to give over. The traditional subjects of salary, seniority and sex seem to have been abandoned in favour of this futile interline warfare.

The world recession, coupled with the classic failure of British Airways to contain their costs, has brought them to bankruptcy and beyond. As has happened before throughout British aviation history, they need subsidies over the bad patch to enable them to survive until the next upswing. The process of cutting back, closing down routes and selling off aircraft and assets is already overdone and can now only prejudice their recovery and compromise the day when the government can present the bill for repayment. British taxpayers get a lot for their money anyway. They get a first in supersonic flight, even if they consider Concorde to be a white elephant and a silly national extravagance. They get a lead in all-weather autoland operations. Over the years they have had massive support for home aircraft production, and British Airways cannot be blamed entirely for the demise of that industry. Along with the noise and air pollution at London Airport, British Airways has turned Heathrow into the country's major port, bringing employment and business and great profit to the region. In addition, it is a pretty good outfit to fly with. I suppose private enterprise could do all that and survive the competition of Europe's nationalised airlines, not to mention the even more heavily subsidised Middle and Far East lines, and the cut-throat competition of the American carriers on the Atlantic. I beg leave to doubt it.

Then there's the business of the third London Airport. Unable to decide among the various options, the British fiddle the time away on ever more expensive and futile public enquiries. The place for the third London Airport is Heathrow. The very first plan back in the 1950s, for a box of runways leaving a tiny patch in the middle for the terminals, was a planning disaster, and London Airport suffers from it to this day. The runway box has long since been broken up, and now only three runways remain, and that has eased the deadlock, allowing some expansion to the west. But that is not enough. What has to be done is to re-site the main east–west runway 10L–28R, by building another further to the north, thus at one move doubling air traffic handling capacity by permitting parallel runway usage and giving virtually unlimited surface access. Heathrow could then go on to being a major airport, not just a sorry mess.

While the aeroplanes get bigger the crew numbers fall. I don't mean the number of cabin attendants. Of necessity their numbers grow inexorably, together with crew costs. Nothing I say will prevent the now traditional three-man crew being reduced to two. The American presidential inquiry on the subject, to which the American airline pilots were committed, were in favour of the two-man crew. Where they lead, we follow.

One of the preoccupations of my time in training, was incapacity and, during every competency check, one crew member dropped out for a spell, leaving the others to demonstrate their ability to survive and complete the flight. This section of the check should get more interesting for those who write the simulator routines. It wouldn't do to make that bit too difficult and get too many failures. The old-timers from the days of real aviation before the Second World War will be thrilled to see that the wheel has come almost full circle. The specialist crew members, with the captain in the role of commander, have come and gone. The three-man crew, with the captain as a working member replaced them, to give way in turn to the one man and a boy concept.

The aviators need not expect too much sympathy from the travelling public, who see them rather as spoilt darlings anyway. Passengers are often surprised on the long flights when the crews slip and desert them, instead of flogging all the way through as they have to do. The trainers will have to stop using the term 'a one-man band' as a term of abuse for the overconfident pilot who takes everything upon himself and fails to make use of his crew. To be a one-man band will be essential if the flight is to be completed safely.

'Eternal vigilance is the price of safety', quoth the Air Marshal. I don't know if it was before or after that when he took off with the control locks in. He was such a marvellous pilot he succeeded in flying the aeroplane in that condition and even got it back in one piece. This story may be apocryphal. There are many like it. If any such thing were to happen to your ordinary run of the mill pilot, he would almost certainly, finish up in a smoking heap. (Ordinary, run of the mill pilots may feel entitled to say that they wouldn't have taken off in that condition in the first place.) Then there would have to be an investigation. Accident investigations are a strange mixture comprising, on the one hand, earnest seekers after truth and, on the other, those who feel their best interests are served by concealing the truth, or at least the unpalatable bits.

The public takes an intense interest in aircraft accidents and their interest is reflected in the media. Even if at times this interest is counterproductive, it is no bad thing. It is vitally important to aviation to understand the causes of accidents in order to avoid them. I am not a statistical man but I can say that enormous improvements have been made in flight safety and accidents are, fortunately, rare nowadays. The greatest single improvement has come about in the design of the aeroplanes themselves. They are far more fitted for their task than their predecessors were and, consequently, are much easier to fly. So we can confidently continue to expect a fairly clean record, apart from the human tendency to err. 'What we need now', said one of my fellow captains, 'is better human beings'.

Captain Jack Nicholl, who was training manager for BOAC at one stage, used to pose some interesting questions. One question went like this: 'How do you arrive at a suitable punishment for a pilot who has had an accident?' Then he would take a step back. 'Why do you want to punish him anyway? Chances are he didn't do it deliberately'. Then he would return to the first question, assuming the second had been answered satisfactorily. This led inexorably to the punishment itself. How was it graded? What should be the scale of penalties? Should punishment be given according to the amount of damage caused or perhaps, on a scale commensurate with the number of the dead? And, if the dead included VIPs, say a football team, should the penalties be increased to take account of rank or popularity, or some other criterion? I didn't attempt an answer to Jack's questions. I felt sure he didn't expect one, but waited confidently for him to answer himself. As he never did, I assumed the questions to be rhetorical.

Yet airline managers and newspaper reporters and even members of the public are often ready to answer. Only recently, I read in my newspaper about a pilot who neglected to refuel his aeroplane and, as a direct consequence, ran out of fuel before he reached his destination. He did what is called a dead stick landing in a cornfield on the approach to the aerodrome. Despite the fact that the air navigation order and its heirs and successors ascribe to the pilot as his first duty the need to ensure 'sufficient fuel for the flight', it was reported that the passengers were so pleased with him that they thought he ought to be given a medal. It reminded me of another case in the Gulf that I thought I might be called upon to investigate but, fortunately that duty fell elsewhere. Our hero took off and was flying along happily when both engines stopped. He was forced to ditch. The sole passenger was trapped inside the aeroplane and the pilot, who was something of an aquatic type, freed him and both were rescued. The Arabic press hailed him as a hero, as indeed he was and, as the investigation revealed nothing further, the aeroplane being at the bottom of the sea, the matter was left at that. I did hear that the engine manufacturers, or at least the rep. they sent out, weren't too happy lest the fault be put down to a shortcoming of their engines. But accidents are seldom due to one single cause or failure. It is, most usually, a combination of circumstances. In writing or talking of other people's accidents, there is always the possibility of getting it slightly wrong, but if you stay with first-hand experience, then what you write or say must have some relevance.

I was lucky enough, even including the period of war-like activity, not to be involved in an aircraft accident, but there were one or two close calls. On three occasions, as a commercial pilot, I was involved in what is called an air miss. The term is self-descriptive. The last one was fairly close to the end of my flying career and, indeed, bid fair to close it there and then.

We were approaching Yalova, a place south-east of Istanbul, heading west for London. Air traffic control at Istanbul, if not brilliant, is generally fairly good and they had recently acquired a new radar and so were becoming less reliant on procedural clearances and were changing over to radar procedures. When we left Ankara control and established contact with Istanbul, we requested re-clearance to the next higher flight level, a step of four thousand feet. After some delay clearance was granted and we opened up the taps to grind our way upward. I don't suppose we were complying with the minimum rate of climb that is implicit in such a clearance, so the TriStar at altitude is only good for about two to three hundred feet a minute, but there was no urgency, merely the requirement to report leaving and reaching the assigned levels. Unknown to us, however, a TriStar from the opposite direction was cruising level slap bang at our mid-altitude. He, too, was working Istanbul, but on a different frequency, the area being split up into sectors around the city.

The first thing we knew of him was his east-bound call over Yalova. Before the full implication had sunk in, the great dark bulk of a TriStar grew out of the darkness and passed a foot or so overhead. A miss, they say, is as good as a mile. Nevertheless, a detached listener might have detected a tremor in my voice as I reported the air miss. I knew the captain of the opposite direction flight, but whether he'd seen us was not immediately clear as he was acting cagey. The air traffic controller was overcome with remorse and apology and there seemed little point in railing at him, other than the giving of formal notice so that he could prepare his report. As we drew apart at better than a thousand miles per hour, some six hundred people, comfortably eating or sleeping, continued on their journey unaware of their horrifying brush with the angel of death.

It was an outfit very used to air misses. The flight safety group devoted much of their time to it. Over Saudi Arabia the flights to Cairo were often endangered by the lack of air traffic control. For all their vast and growing wealth, the Saudis neglected to install the communications network necessary to exercise control and we had to recourse to the buddy watch system, broadcasting all position reports and rearranging flight levels to avoid collision. Saudi turned a deaf ear to all protests. Then, in the chaos of Egyptian air traffic control from Luxor to Cairo, the Saudi experience paled into insignificance. So nothing came of my report, which was left to gather dust somewhere in a file.

It was Napoleon who liked his commanders to be lucky. Airline passengers need to share his views. The manufacturers have made the aeroplanes safer by making them easier to fly and giving greater system redundancy. You have to have a lot of failures to get right down to running on the rims. (Wheels and rims are the exception, however.) There are unscrupulous operators and inefficient servicing organisations who take advantage of system redundancy to go right back to square one and operate the aeroplane so that one more failure will produce an emergency situation. But, mostly, the engineers have become adept at picking up the failures before they occur and engines get changed and overhauled before they have a chance to fail in the air.

In a way, the trainers try to do the same thing with pilots. On the simulator, they try to force mistakes in order to correct them, confining failures to the ground. This is not an enjoyable process but a worthwhile one. Then there is a whole flight safety industry that produces reams of paperwork, horror comics, cautionary tales and recommendations too numerous to mention. In addition to every major airline having a safety group of some kind, governments, regulating bodies and international organisations all join in. To be fair, they do have a contribution to make, even if only to alert the aviators. 'In vain is the trap set in sight of the bird.' If you want to get something done in aviation, and you can hang a flight safety label on it, the chances are you will get it through. But above all, the aeroplanes are better, easier to fly and, therefore, safer.

I have another regret, but only a minor one, I didn't get to fly the Jumbo, the 747. When I refer to flying an aeroplane, I don't mean just sitting in the seat and laying hands on the controls, I mean qualifying on it, getting a recognised authority to endorse my ATPL with the type. Really flying it, as P1, pilot in charge. I asked Jumbo Jarvis what it was like. 'It's just like flying a Tiger Moth, Jeff', he said. 'You fly it just as you would a Tiger Moth, it's that simple'. That's easy, I thought. That's where I came in.

Index